The Complete Rival® Roaster Oven Cookbook

THE COMPLETE

ROASTER OVEN
COOKBOOK

Family Favorites for Every Day of the Week!

From the Test Kitchens of
THE HOLMES GROUP

Pascoe Publishing, Inc.
Rocklin, California

Published in the United States by
Pascoe Publishing, Inc.
Rocklin, California
http://www.pascoepublishing.com

ISBN: 1-929862-15-6

02   03   04   05   10   9   8   7   6   5   4   3   2   1

Printed in the United States of America

TABLE OF CONTENTS

ACKNOWLEDGMENTS

The Holmes Group gratefully acknowledges the efforts of Tasha Ann Sevland, who developed, tested, tasted and polished the outstanding recipes in this cookbook. Tasha spent many hours on this project and her work is truly appreciated.

8

INTRODUCTION

If you've never tried using a Rival® Roaster Oven before, get ready for a delicious journey! Meats and poultry roasted in the Roaster Oven are more tender and moist and have better flavor than any other method of cooking because all of the natural juices are locked into the foods as they roast. And, if you look beyond poultry, beef, pork and seafood, you'll find that the Roaster Oven creates some amazingly delicious side dishes, desserts and appetizers, too!

Now, more than ever, families are enjoying mealtime together. Using your Rival® Roaster Oven to create one-dish meals, stews, soups and casseroles is a great way to save time in the kitchen. It's also easy to double a recipe. Just serve half and freeze the remaining meal for another evening. Or, prepare a perfect potluck main dish for your friends and family. Use your Roaster Oven to make breads, bake pies and roast vegetables—the list of recipe ideas is endless! We invite you to enjoy the scrumptious recipes inside this book, from our kitchen to yours.

Chapter 1

USING YOUR RIVAL® ROASTER OVEN: HINTS & TIPS

In our test kitchens we share food preparation and roasting hints with each other, just as you might with your friends at work or your neighbor next door. With that in mind, we'd like to share some hints that will help ease your preparation of foods and allow you to get the most from your Rival® Roaster Oven:

- If you are going to roast or bake foods that might stick, lightly coat the cooking pan with nonstick cooking spray. This really helps when it's time to clean up!

- Most of these recipes can be doubled for the larger-sized Rival® Roaster Ovens. Check the recipe to determine whether you will need a roasting rack. And make sure you are using the correct baking pan for the recipe.

- Some foods, such as breads baked in loaf pans, can be placed side by side on the roasting rack, as space allows.

- *Baking.* You'll find several recipes in this book for baking. When using a baking pan, always place the pan on the roasting rack. Do not place baking pans on the bottom of the cooking pan. Metal pans are recommended for use in the Roaster Oven, as they provide better heat transfer and browning.

- The Rival® Roaster Oven roasts and bakes at approximately the same temperatures and in the same time as a standard roaster oven.

- Significant amounts of heat escape whenever the lid is removed. Avoid removing the lid as much as possible, as this extends the required cooking time.

- Do not place food or liquid directly into the body of the Roaster Oven.

- The best flavors come from fresh herbs and spices. If possible, try to use fresh ingredients for roasting. The flavors develop during the moist cooking process more than they would in a dry heat method of cooking.

- *Browning.* Because the Roaster Oven does not brown in the same fashion as an oven, prepare chicken and turkey with a browning sauce, oil, butter or a dusting of paprika. Some meats, such as chicken pieces and beef stew pieces, are best when browned for a few minutes in a bit of oil in a sauté pan and then added to the Roaster Oven. For a dark roasted, crispy poultry skin do not add liquids (with the exception of the basting butter or oil) until the last 30 minutes of roasting.

◆ Roasting creates such incredibly moist meats and poultry that you may find the meat literally falls from the bones. If this happens, use a slotted spoon or ladle to scoop up the meat and spoon any juices or sauce over the cooked meat.

◆ Tender cuts of meat are best suited for roasting. The time guides given in this chapter are for use with tender cuts, such as sirloin and standing rib roasts.

◆ *Slow Cooking.* When roasting less tender cuts of meat use the slow cooking method of roasting, adding liquids such as chicken or beef broth. When slow cooking, it is not necessary to stir the meat and it is best to keep the lid on to retain the heat and moisture. To convert a standard recipe to slow cooking, heat to 250°F temperature and slow cook 1½ hours for every 30 minutes designated in the recipe.

◆ *Cooking Temperatures.* Internal cooking temperatures are very important when cooking meat and poultry. Because harmful bacteria can remain present in foods that are undercooked, use a temperature fork or meat thermometer when roasting. Insert the thermometer into the thickest portion of the meat and refer to the following guides (times indicated are approximate and should be used as a guideline only).

Meat Cooking Guide

MEAT	RARE	MEDIUM	WELL DONE
BEEF	145°F	160°F	170°F
PORK		160°F	170°F
LAMB		160°F	170°F
SMOKED HAM			
Cook before eating			160°F
Fully cooked			140°F
POULTRY			
Roasting Chicken			180°F
Turkey			180°F

NOTE: Rare pork, ham or poultry is not recommended.

Meat Time & Temperature Roasting Guide

MEAT	WEIGHT (LBS.)	TEMPERATURE	MIN./LB.
BEEF ROASTS			
Standing Rib	4 to 6	325°F	20 to 25
Sirloin Tip	3 to 5	350°F	20 to 25
Tenderloin	3½ to 4	450°F	8 to 12
Pot Roast	4 to 6	300°F	30 to 40
Corned Beef	3½ to 4	300°F	15 to 20
LAMB			
Leg	5 to 8	350°F	25
Shoulder, boneless	3 to 4	350°F	25
PORK			
Loin Roast	3 to 5	350°F	25 to 30
Rolled Shoulder	4 to 6	350°F	25 to 30
Chops	4 to 5	325°F	15 to 20
Country-Style Ribs	8 to 10	450°F	to brown
		reduce temp. to 250°F	15 to 20

MEAT	WEIGHT (LBS.)	TEMPERATURE	MIN./LB.
SMOKED HAM			
Bone-in, shankless	10 to 15	325°F	20 to 25
Boneless	8 to 12	325°F	15 to 20
Fully Cooked	5 to 10	325°F	13 to 28
VEAL			
Loin	4 to 6	325°F	30 to 35
Shoulder	3 to 5	325°F	30 to 35
POULTRY			
Chicken, whole	3½ to 5	350°F	15 to 17
Chicken, whole	6 to 8	350°F	18 to 20
Chicken, pieces	6 to 8	350°F	8 to 10
Turkey, prebasted	10 to 14	375°F	12 to 17
Turkey, prebasted	14 to 22	375°F	13 to 18
Turkey, fresh	10 to 14	350°F	15 to 20

FOOD	TEMPERATURE	BAKING TIME (MIN.)
Muffins	425°F	15 to 20
Quick Bread	375°F	65 to 75
Yeast Bread	400°F	40 to 45
Yeast Rolls	400°F	18 to 20
Cookies	350°F	11 to 13
Brownies	350°F	25 to 30
Cupcakes	350°F	25 to 30
Sheet Cake	350°F	40 to 45
Pound Cake	350°F	50 to 60
Bundt Cake	350°F	50 to 60
Cheesecake	325°F	50 to 60
Fruit Pie	425°F	45 to 50
Custard Pie	350°F	50 to 60
Pastry Shell	425°F	10 to 13
Pizza (9-inch)	425°F	20 to 25
Baked Potatoes	350° to 400°F	50 to 60
Sweet Potatoes	350° to 400°F	55 to 65
Scalloped Potatoes	350°F	75 to 90
Winter Squash	400°F	45 to 60
Baked Apples	350°F	35 to 45

NOTE: Always preheat the Roaster Oven prior to baking.

Chapter Two

AROUND-THE-CLOCK APPETIZERS & SNACKS

Your Rival® Roaster Oven is the perfect party host! Try any of the following recipes for your next gathering and sit back to receive the compliments. And you may double most recipes to make your job even easier. For a casual party, try *Asian Spareribs* or *Spicy Island Chicken Skewers*. An elegant dinner party calls for *Zippy Shrimp* or *Spinach & Artichoke Roll-Ups*. And for those days when your family is attached to the football game and looking for snacks, try *Garlic Rosemary Wings, Tuscany Bread Sticks* or *Hot & Spicy Chicken Wings*. It's always the right time for appetizers and snacks!

ASIAN SPARERIBS

The fresh ginger and garlic, combined with the hoisin sauce, offer an Oriental twist to these spareribs. Serve with pineapple and melon salad as a flavorful complement.

This recipe can be doubled for the 18 or 20 quart Roaster Oven.

3-4 lbs. lean pork spareribs

2 large cloves garlic, minced

1 Tbsp. fresh ginger, minced

4 green onions, thinly sliced

1/4 cup brown sugar

4 Tbsp. hoisin sauce

1 Tbsp. sesame oil

2 tsp. five spice powder

1 tsp. salt

Cut the sparerib racks to fit into the cooking pan. In a small bowl, combine the garlic, ginger, green onions, brown sugar, hoisin sauce, sesame oil, five-spice powder and salt and blend well. Sprinkle the ribs with a bit of additional salt and brush with the sauce. Place the ribs in the cooking pan. Roast at 350°F for 1½-2 hours. Allow the ribs to cool slightly and cut into individual pieces to serve. Serves 10-12.

GARLIC ROSEMARY WINGS

10-15 chicken wings

3 Tbsp. extra-virgin olive oil

2 cloves garlic, minced

2 tsp. dried rosemary

1/2 cup fresh lemon juice

1 tsp. black pepper

1 tsp. salt

The essence of rosemary mingles with garlic to give these wings a kick!

Cut off the tip end of each wing and discard. Preheat the Roaster Oven to 350°F. In a small bowl, combine the olive oil, garlic, rosemary, lemon juice, pepper and salt. Place the wings in the bottom of the cooking pan and pour the sauce over the wings. Turn the wings to coat thoroughly. Roast for 1-1½ hours, or until the chicken has reached the correct internal temperature. Serves 5-6.

GREEK GARLIC BREAD

Lemon juice is an unusual addition to this bread, but it pairs well with the garlic.

1 loaf French bread, unsliced

3/4 cup butter, melted

4 tsp. fresh lemon juice

1 Tbsp. lemon peel, grated

2 cloves garlic, minced

1/4 tsp. black pepper

Preheat the Roaster Oven to 400°F. Slice the bread in half horizontally. In a small bowl, combine the butter, lemon juice, lemon peel, garlic and pepper and mix well. Brush the seasoned butter over the two halves of bread. Wrap the bread in aluminum foil and place in the cooking pan. Cover and bake for 15-20 minutes. To serve, slice each half of bread into 12 slices. Serves 20-24.

TUSCANY BREAD STICKS

3 Tbsp. extra-virgin olive oil

3 cloves garlic, minced

1/4 tsp. salt

1/2 tsp. black pepper

1 loaf French bread, cut into 24 slices, 1/2-inch thick

Olive oil and garlic will remind diners of the warm Tuscan region of Italy.

In a small bowl, combine the olive oil, garlic, salt and pepper. Cover tightly and refrigerate for up to 24 hours. Arrange the bread slices in the bottom of the cooking pan, and brush both sides with the oil mixture. Cover and bake at 350°F for 15 minutes, or until very lightly toasted.

*Bake the bread in multiple batches when using the 6, 8, or 10 quart Roaster Oven.

SPICY ISLAND CHICKEN SKEWERS

*A perfect beginning
to a relaxed
weekend meal.*

4 skinless, boneless chicken breasts

12 bamboo skewers, soaked in water 30 minutes, drained

1 cup extra-virgin olive oil

1 cup fresh lime juice

4 large cloves garlic, pressed

2 tsp. salt

2 tsp. hot pepper sauce

Cut each chicken breast lengthwise into 3 strips. Thread
the chicken onto the skewers and place them in a large
baking dish. Mix the olive oil, lime juice, garlic, salt and hot
pepper sauce in a bowl and whisk vigorously. Pour the
marinade over the chicken and refrigerate for 1 hour or up
to 24 hours in the refrigerator. Place the chicken skewers
on the bottom of the cooking pan and discard the unused
marinade. Cover and bake at 350°F for 25-30 minutes, or
until the internal temperature of the chicken is correct.
Serves 12.

ITALIAN SAUSAGE-STUFFED GREEN PEPPERS

1 lb. sweet Italian sausages, casings removed

1 cup white onion, chopped

1/3 cup fresh parsley, minced

1 cup fine bread crumbs, dried

2 large eggs, beaten

1 tsp. ground black pepper

3/4 tsp. salt

5 medium-sized green peppers, halved lengthwise, seeded and cored

1 cup mozzarella cheese, shredded

Melted mozzarella cheese adds a rich, mellow note to these peppers.

Lightly coat the cooking pan with cooking spray. Combine the sausages, onion, parsley, bread crumbs, eggs, pepper and salt in a large bowl and mix well. Spoon equal portions of the stuffing into each pepper half, mounding slightly. Place the peppers in the cooking pan. Cover and cook at 350°F for 35-60 minutes. During the last 5 minutes of cooking, sprinkle the mozzarella cheese on top of each pepper. The peppers are done when the sausage stuffing has reached the proper cooking temperature and the cheese is melted and hot.

*This recipe can be doubled for the 18 or 20 quart Roaster Oven.

25

ZIPPY SHRIMP

This name says it all —spicy and hot!

juice of 2 lemons

2 cloves garlic, minced

2 tsp. Tabasco™ sauce

1 tsp. chili powder

1/4 tsp. dried red pepper, crushed

1/2 tsp. salt

1/4 cup vegetable oil

4 lbs. uncooked shrimp, peeled and deveined

*This recipe can be doubled for the 18 or 20 quart Roaster Oven.

Combine the lemon juice, garlic, hot sauce, chili powder, red pepper, salt and oil in a large bowl. Whisk the ingredients together. Add the shrimp and allow the shrimp to marinate for at least 1 hour or up to 12 hours. Lightly coat the bottom of the cooking pan with cooking spray and arrange the shrimp on the bottom of the pan. Cover and cook at 425°F for 25-35 minutes.

SPINACH & ARTICHOKE ROLL UPS

10 oz. frozen chopped spinach, thawed and squeezed dry

1/2 cup marinated artichokes, drained

8 oz. cream cheese, at room temperature

1/2 cup mayonnaise

1 tsp. salt

1/2 tsp. black pepper

1/2 cup green onions, chopped

4 9-inch flour tortillas

An easy appetizer that can be made a day ahead and heated just before your guests arrive.

This recipe can be doubled for the 18 or 20 quart Roaster Oven.

Combine the spinach, artichokes, cream cheese, mayonnaise, salt, pepper and green onions in a medium bowl and mix well. Spread the mixture evenly on each flour tortilla, leaving a 1/2-inch border around the edges. On 1 tortilla, fold the 1/2-inch border down on all sides, starting at the bottom of the tortilla and finish rolling the tortilla completely. Repeat the process for the remaining three tortillas. Wrap each tortilla individually in plastic wrap and refrigerate for at least 1 hour. Remove the tortillas from the plastic wrap and slice off the unfilled ends of each tortilla. Cut each tortilla into slices 1-inch wide and arrange the slices on the bottom of the cooking pan. Cover and bake at 350°F for 5 minutes or until the Roll-Ups are warmed through and tender. Serves 18, 2 pieces per person.

HOT & SPICY CHICKEN WINGS

The first bite of these tasty wings gives away the ranch dressing secret!

1/4 cup butter or margarine, melted
1/2 cup bottled hot sauce
1 oz. pkg. powdered ranch dressing mix
2 lbs. chicken wings, tips removed

*This recipe can be doubled for the 18 or 20 quart Roaster Oven.

In a small bowl, combine the butter and hot sauce. Sprinkle the powdered ranch dressing mix on a large plate. Dip the chicken wings in the sauce mixture then roll in the dressing mix. Spread the chicken on to the bottom of the cooking pan. Cover and bake at 350°F 16-30 minutes, or until the internal temperature is correct. Serves 12-14.

Chapter Three

THE BEST OF BREAKFAST RECIPES

The best recipe for starting your day right is by eating a good breakfast. The recipes in this chapter will allow you to prepare and serve a hearty breakfast or brunch any day of the week. Skip that fast-food breakfast and instead prepare *Bacon & Cheddar Breakfast Pizza*—it will disappear in a flash! Bake any of our delicious scones and grab coffee to go. Several of these recipes can also be frozen and reheated—simply seal in a freezer bag and use within one week.

Weekend mornings call for a leisurely breakfast for the entire family and we suggest the ever-popular *Rival® Roaster French Toast* for kids of all ages. If you really want to enjoy the start of the day choose your own syrup and fruit toppings and add a dollop of whipped cream. And if you are entertaining weekend guests, try *Breakfast Peach Delight* or *Sunny Potato Casserole* for an easy way to serve a crowd.

GOOD MORNING ONE-PAN BREAKFAST

Add some fruit and a hot cup of coffee—breakfast is ready!

1 lb. ground sausage patties, cooked and drained

3 cups hominy grits, cooked

1 cup cheddar cheese, grated

3 Tbsp. butter or margarine

1 small white onion, chopped

6 eggs, well-beaten

For the 6, 8, or 10 quart Roaster Oven, decrease the recipe by half and use a small loaf pan.

Lightly grease a 9" x 13" pan. Spread the sausage evenly on the bottom of the pan. Cook the grits according to the package directions (use a microwave to save time, if desired). Add the cheddar cheese and margarine to the cooked grits and stir until the cheese and margarine are melted. Allow the grits to cool slightly. Add the onion. Stir the eggs into the grits. Pour the grits mixture over the sausage. Place the pan on the roasting rack in the cooking pan. Cover and cook at 350°F for 25-30 minutes, or until the eggs are set and cooked through completely. Serves 8-12.

BACON & EGG CASSEROLE

8 slices white bread, toasted and cubed

1/2 cup butter or margarine, melted

2 cups cheddar cheese, grated

2 cups white onion, chopped

8 eggs

1 cup water

5 slices bacon, cooked and crumbled

This cooks into a quiche-like breakfast dish and is a hearty contribution to the first meal of the day.

*For the 6, 8, or 10 quart Roaster Oven, decrease the recipe by half and use a small loaf pan.

Coat a 9" x 13" pan with cooking spray. Place the bread cubes in the pan and pour the butter over them. Sprinkle the grated cheese over the dish and layer the onions over the cheese. In a small bowl, beat the eggs and water until completely blended. Pour the eggs and water over the bread and cheese layer in the pan. Sprinkle the bacon crumbs over all. Place the pan on the roasting rack in the cooking pan. Cover and cook at 350°F for 25-30 minutes, or until the eggs are set and are cooked through completely. Serves 8-12.

BREAKFAST PEACH DELIGHT

A "peachy" way to start the day!

2-29 oz. cans peach halves, drained
1/2 cup honey
1 tsp. ground cinnamon
1/4 cup + 2 Tbsp. brown sugar
1/2 cup butter or margarine, melted
2 cups granola cereal of your choice

For the 6, 8, or 10 quart Roaster Oven, decrease the recipe by half and use a small loaf pan.

Lightly coat a 9" x 13" pan with cooking spray. Arrange the peach halves on the bottom of the pan, cut side up. Sprinkle the peaches with 2 tablespoons of brown sugar. In a separate bowl, combine the honey, cinnamon, ½ cup of brown sugar, butter and granola. Thoroughly mix the ingredients and sprinkle evenly on top of the peaches. Place the pan on the roasting rack in the cooking pan. Cover and cook at 350°F for 25-30 minutes. Serve warm with milk or cream on the side. Serves 8-10.

SUNNY POTATO CASSEROLE

8 frozen hash brown patties, slightly thawed

12 oz. can evaporated milk

2-10.75 oz. cans condensed potato soup

2 cups sharp cheddar cheese, grated

1 cup butter or margarine, melted and divided

3 oz. cornflakes, crushed

A rich, yummy entrée for a weekend brunch.

Lightly grease the bottom and sides of a 9" x 13" pan. Place the hash browns in the bottom of the casserole dish. In a large bowl, combine the milk, soup, cheese and ½ cup of the melted butter. Stir gently until well-combined. Pour the mixture evenly over the hash browns. In a small bowl, combine the crushed cornflakes and ½ cup of butter. Sprinkle evenly over the hash brown mixture. Place the pan on the roasting rack in the cooking pan. Cover and bake at 350°F for 30-40 minutes, or until the hash browns are cooked through and the casserole is bubbly. Serves 8-10.

*For the 6, 8, or 10 quart Roaster Oven, decrease the recipe by half and use a small loaf pan.

33

CINNAMON RAISIN BAKED APPLES

Baked apple slices partner with peanuts, raisins and sweet spices.

For the 6, 8, or 10 quart Roaster Oven, decrease the recipe by half and use a small loaf pan.

6 baking apples, peeled and sliced

1 3/4 cups flour

1/2 cup sugar

1 tsp. cinnamon

1/8 tsp. salt

1 tsp. fresh orange peel, grated

1/4 cup smooth peanut butter

1/2 cup butter or margarine

1/4 cup peanuts, shelled and chopped

1/2 cup raisins

1/2 cup water

1/2 cup orange juice

Arrange the apple slices in the bottom of a lightly greased 9" x 13" pan. Mix together the flour, sugar, cinnamon, salt, orange peel, peanut butter and butter until crumbly. Add the peanuts and raisins and mix again. Sprinkle the crumble mixture over the apples evenly. Mix the water and orange juice together in a small bowl and pour over the apples. Place the pan on the roasting rack in the cooking pan. Cover and bake at 350°F for 50-75 minutes. Serves 6-8.

BACON & CHEDDAR BREAKFAST PIZZA

8 oz. crescent refrigerated rolls

1 lb. bacon, cooked and crumbled

1 cup shredded hash browns, thawed

2 cups cheddar cheese, shredded

4 eggs, beaten

1/4 cup lowfat milk

1/4 tsp. salt

1/2 tsp. black pepper

Everything for breakfast in one easy pizza!

Separate the crescent dough into 8 triangles. Place the triangles in a 9" x 9" pan, pressing the bottom and sides to form a crust. Seal the dough perforations. Spoon the crumbled bacon over the dough and sprinkle the hash browns and cheese over the bacon. In a small bowl, combine the eggs, milk, salt and pepper and blend well. Pour over the pizza. Place the pan on the roasting rack in the cooking pan. Cover and bake at 375°F for 25-35 minutes, or until the eggs are set and cooked through completely. Serves 8.

*For the 6, 8, or 10 quart Roaster Oven, decrease the recipe by half and use a small loaf pan.

RIVAL® ROASTER FRENCH TOAST

This is the perfect Saturday family breakfast! Add maple syrup or a fresh fruit topping.

4 eggs, separated

1/4 cup sugar

2 tsp. vanilla extract

1/2 cup lowfat milk

6 slices bread of your choice

*For the 6, 8, or 10 quart Roaster Oven, decrease the recipe by half and use a small loaf pan.

Preheat the Roaster Oven to 450°F. Lightly coat a 9" x 13" pan with cooking spray. In a small bowl, beat the egg whites until they reach the soft peak stage. In a medium bowl, combine the egg yolks, sugar, vanilla extract and milk. Gently fold the egg whites into the egg yolk mixture. Dip one slice of bread into the egg and milk and place the bread in the pan. Repeat with the remaining slices of bread. Place the pan on the roasting rack in the cooking pan. Cover and bake for 10-15 minutes. Serves 3-4.

SOUR CREAM RAISIN SCONES

4 cups all-purpose flour

2 Tbsp. baking powder

1/2 cup unsalted butter

1/4 cup sour cream

1 cup milk

3/4 cup dark raisins

In a large bowl, sift together the flour and baking powder. Cut the butter into the dry ingredients until the mixture resembles small, coarse crumbs. In a separate bowl, combine the sour cream, milk and raisins. Mix the sour cream mixture into the flour and butter dough until combined thoroughly. Shape into a circle on a floured surface. With a rolling pin, roll the dough out to an even ½ -inch thickness. Cut into small squares (or round shapes, if preferred). Lightly coat a 9" x 13" pan with cooking spray and put the scones in the pan. Place the pan on the roasting rack in the cooking pan. Cover and bake at 425°F for 25-30 minutes, or until the scones are lightly golden in color. Serves 8.

Each mouthful is punctuated by plump, dark raisins. These are best served warm with butter.

For the 6, 8 or 10 quart Roaster Oven, the scone recipe can be decreased by half. Use a 5" x 7" loaf pan or make scones in multiple batches.

DRIED FRUIT SCONES

Use any dried fruit or prepare your own favorite combinations.

2 1/2 cups all purpose flour

3 tsp. baking powder

1/2 cup sugar

6 Tbsp. cold butter, cut into small pieces

1 cup dried fruit (cranberries, apricots, cherries, etc)

2 eggs, beaten

1 cup sour cream

For the 6, 8 or 10 quart Roaster Oven, the scone recipe can be decreased by half. Use a small loaf pan or make scones in multiple batches.

Preheat the Roaster Oven to 425°F. Lightly grease a 9" x 13" pan; set aside. In a large bowl, sift together the flour and baking powder. Blend in the sugar and mix again. Add the butter in small amounts, mixing with the flour, until the dough resembles small crumbs. Add the dried fruit and mix again. Stir in the eggs and sour cream and blend completely. Turn the dough out onto a floured surface and shape into a circle. Roll out the dough with a floured rolling pin to an even ½-inch thickness. Cut the scones in your desired shape (squares, triangles, or circles), and place in the baking pan. Place the pan on the roasting rack in the cooking pan. Cover and cook at 425°F for 25-35 minutes, or until the scones are lightly golden in color. Serves 8.

IRISH OATMEAL SCONES

2 cups all purpose flour

2 Tbsp. baking powder

1/3 cup sugar

3/4 cup chilled, unsalted butter, cut into pieces

1 1/3 cups rolled oats, regular or instant

1/2 cup dried fruit (cranberries, apricots, cherries, etc)

1/2 cup milk

Preheat the Roaster Oven to 425°F. Lightly grease a 9" x 13" pan. Sift together the flour and baking powder in a large bowl. Stir in the sugar and add the butter in small amounts. Cut the butter into the flour until the dough resembles small crumbs. Mix in the rolled oats and dried fruit and stir well. Add the milk (note: more milk may be required to make a soft dough, based on the humidity in your region). Turn out the dough onto a floured surface and form a circle. Roll out with a floured rolling pin to an even ½ -inch thickness. Cut the scones into shapes of your choice (squares, triangles, circles, etc.) and place the scones in the baking pan. Place the pan on the roasting rack in the cooking pan. Cover and cook at 425°F for 25-35 minutes, or until scones are lightly golden in color. Serves 8.

Serve with a warm cup o' tea.

For the 6, 8 or 10 quart Roaster Oven, the scone recipe can be decreased by half. Use a small loaf pan or make scones in multiple batches.

SUPER NUTTY GRANOLA

Crunchy, flavorful mix that works well as a cereal or a snack!

1 cup brown sugar

1/2 cup water

6 cups rolled oats

2 cups pecans, walnuts or almonds, chopped

*This recipe may be doubled for the 18 or 20 quart Roaster Oven. Cook in two batches.

Lightly coat the cooking pan with nonstick cooking spray. Preheat the Roaster Oven to 275°F. In a large bowl, combine the sugar and water and mix well. Add the oats and nuts and blend again. Spread the granola evenly in the cooking pan. Cover and cook for 50-60 minutes. Allow the granola to cool completely and store in an airtight container. Serves 12.

QUICK & CHEESY BREAKFAST CASSEROLE

6 eggs

2 cups milk

6 cups bread, cubed

1 1/2 cups cheddar cheese, shredded

A few tasty ingredients and a few simple steps result in delectable goodness.

Preheat the Roaster Oven to 325°F. Lightly grease a 9" x 13" baking pan. In a large bowl, combine the eggs and milk with a whisk. When well blended, fold in the bread cubes. Pour the mixture into the baking pan and sprinkle the cheese evenly on top. Place the pan on the roasting rack in the cooking pan. Cover and cook for 45 to 60 minutes, or until the center is set. Serves 8.

*For the 6, 8 or 10 quart Roaster Oven, decrease the recipe by half and use a small loaf pan.

41

Chapter 4

SOUPS & STEWS FOR ANY DAY OF THE WEEK

There is nothing better on a cold winter's evening than coming home to the aroma of a hearty soup or stew simmering in the Roaster Oven. Whether you prefer a hearty meat and vegetable stew or opt for the silky richness of a cheese or cream-based soup you will find that the Rival® Roaster Oven does the job perfectly every time.

Try *Homestyle Beef Stew, Classic Minestrone* or *Blue Collar Bean & Sausage Soup* for a middle-of-the-week meal. To complete the entrée add a dense bread, such as pumpernickel or dark rye. For a satisfying first course or to enliven a weekend meal try *Steaming Shellfish Stew* or *White Wine & Rosemary Lamb Stew.* When you have about 15 minutes and a hungry family, select *Grandmother's Quick Chicken & Rice Soup* to save the day.

ZESTY CORN CHOWDER

Herbs and spices pep up this hearty corn chowder.

3 cups skim milk

2 cups chicken broth

2 cups frozen whole kernel corn

1 sweet red pepper, cored, seeded and diced

1 green pepper, cored, seeded and diced

1/2 tsp. cayenne pepper

1 tsp. garlic powder

1 tsp. onion powder

1/2 tsp. coarse black pepper

1 cup white onion, chopped

1 cup celery, chopped

2 Tbsp. butter or margarine

*This recipe can be doubled for the 18 or 20 quart Roaster Oven.

Place the milk, chicken broth, corn and peppers in the cooking pan. Heat the Roaster Oven to 250°F and stir in the cayenne pepper, garlic powder, onion powder, pepper and onion. Mix lightly. Add the celery and butter and stir again. Cover and simmer for 25-35 minutes. Serves 6.

ROASTED VEGETABLE SOUP

2 Tbsp. extra-virgin olive oil

1 tsp. salt

1/2 tsp. ground black pepper

1 tsp. dried rosemary

1 lb. fresh asparagus, cleaned and sliced into 1-inch pieces

1 small yellow squash, cleaned and diced

1 red onion, quartered

1 red bell pepper, cored, seeded and cubed

2 cups whole fresh mushrooms, cleaned and cut into fourths

6 cups chicken broth

Combine the oil, salt, pepper and rosemary in a large bowl. Add the vegetables and stir well to coat. Place the vegetables in the cooking pan. Roast at 450°F for 30 minutes, stirring the vegetables every 10 minutes. Reduce the heat to 250°F. Cover and add the chicken broth. Allow the soup to simmer for 10 minutes. Serves 6.

Substitute any fresh, seasonal vegetables in this lovely soup.

This recipe can be doubled for the 18 or 20 quart Roaster Oven.

STEAMING SHELLFISH STEW

Clams, shrimp and crab are a heavenly combination. Enjoy this stew with a hearty sourdough bread.

*This recipe can be doubled for the 18 or 20 quart Roaster Oven.

1 Tbsp. extra virgin olive oil

1 medium white onion, chopped

2 cloves garlic, pressed or minced

3 oz. can clams, chopped or minced, liquid reserved

6 oz. can white crab, drained and rinsed

1 lb. fresh shrimp, cooked

10.75 oz. can sodium-reduced tomato soup

2 cups water

1/4 cup fresh parsley, minced

1 tsp. freshly ground black pepper

1/2 tsp. dried basil, crushed

Pour the oil into the cooking pan. Heat the Roaster Oven to 375°F. When the oil is hot, but not smoking, add the onion, garlic, clams and crab. Stir and cook for 5 minutes. Reduce the temperature to 250°F and add the shrimp, tomato soup, water, parsley, pepper and basil. Cover and allow the stew to simmer for 25 minutes. Serve hot or warm with thick slices of sourdough bread. Makes 2 hearty dinner servings or 4 luncheon servings.

WHITE WINE & ROSEMARY LAMB STEW

1/4 cup extra-virgin olive oil

3 lbs. lamb, cut into 2-inch cubes

1 bay leaf

1 Tbsp. dried rosemary

2 cloves garlic, minced

2 cups chicken broth

1 cup white wine

28 oz. can crushed tomatoes

2 medium onions, chopped

1/4 tsp. salt

1/2 tsp. black pepper

The wine and tomato sauce adds rich character to the lamb and spices.

*This recipe can be doubled for the 18 or 20 quart Roaster Oven.

Heat the oil in a large sauté pan. Add the lamb cubes and sauté for 1 minute on each side. Place the lamb in the bottom of the cooking pan, along with the browned bits from the bottom of the sauté pan. Add the bay leaf, rosemary, garlic, chicken broth, white wine, crushed tomatoes, onions, salt and pepper and stir to mix well. Cover and cook at 350°F until the stew comes to a boil. Reduce the heat to 250°F and simmer for 1 hour. Remove the bay leaf before serving. Serves 4.

GOLDEN CHEDDAR & HAM CHOWDER

Thick, creamy soup for a cold winter's evening.

This recipe can be doubled for the 18 or 20 quart Roaster Oven.

1/4 cup butter or margarine, melted

1/4 cup all-purpose flour

2 cups lowfat milk

2 cups cheddar cheese, shredded

2 cups water

2 baking potatoes, peeled, cubed and cooked

1 cup carrots, sliced

1 cup celery, sliced

1 cup white onion, chopped

1 cup whole kernel corn (you may use canned or frozen corn, thawed, as preferred)

2 cups fully cooked ham, cubed

Preheat the Roaster Oven to 250°F. Combine the melted butter and flour in the bottom of the cooking pan. Blend completely. Add the milk and stir completely until no lumps remain. When the soup base is well-blended, add the cheddar cheese, ½ cup at a time, stirring constantly. The soup should be thickened and smooth, and the cheese completely melted. Add the water, potatoes, carrots, celery, onion, corn and ham and stir again. Reduce the heat to 200°F and allow the chowder to simmer for 15 minutes. Add salt and pepper to taste, if desired. Serve with cornbread for a complete meal. Serves 4.

CREAMY CHEESE & BROCCOLI SOUP

1/2 cup butter or margarine, melted

1/2 cup all-purpose flour

5 cups water

10 oz. frozen broccoli cuts, thawed

1 tsp. garlic powder

1 tsp. parsley

1/4 tsp. salt

1/2 tsp. black pepper

1 white onion, chopped

8 oz. processed cheese, shredded

1 pint light cream

If you like broccoli with melted cheese, try this rich and delicious soup.

*This recipe can be doubled for the 18 or 20 quart Roaster Oven.

In the bottom of the cooking pan, blend the butter and flour until completely mixed. Heat the Roaster Oven to 350°F. Add the water and blend until no lumps remain. Add the broccoli, garlic powder, parsley, salt and pepper. Cover and bring the soup to a full boil. Stir and reduce the temperature to 250°F. Add the onion, cheese and cream, stirring to melt the cheese and blend the ingredients. Simmer the soup for 10-15 minutes and serve while hot. Serves 6.

RED POTATO SOUP

Quick and easy for a late night supper.

3 cups red potatoes, cooked and mashed

2 cups chicken broth

1 tsp. dried rosemary

1/2 tsp. salt

1 clove garlic, minced

1 cup milk

*This recipe can be doubled for the 18 or 20 quart Roaster Oven.

Combine the potatoes, chicken broth, rosemary, salt, garlic and milk in the cooking pan. Stir well to blend. Cover and heat the Roaster Oven to 250°F. Simmer the soup for 30-40 minutes, stirring occasionally. Serve warm. Serves 2-3.

GRANDMOTHER'S QUICK CHICKEN & RICE SOUP

2 cups chicken, cooked and cubed

4 cups chicken broth

1 cup quick-cooking rice

1 cup water

1 Tbsp. dried parsley

10 oz. frozen mixed vegetables

1/4 tsp. salt

1/2 tsp. black pepper

Homemade flavor in half the time of traditional soup.

Combine the chicken and broth in the cooking pan. Cover and cook at 350°F until the soup reaches a full boil. Add the rice, water, parsley, frozen vegetables, salt and pepper and decrease the heat to 250°F. Allow the soup to simmer for 15 minutes, stirring occasionally, and serve immediately. Serves 2-4.

*This recipe can be doubled for the 18 or 20 quart Roaster Oven.

51

BLUE COLLAR BEAN & SAUSAGE SOUP

This soup makes a working man's meal!

1 1/2 lbs. spicy Italian sausage, sliced into 1/2-inch pieces

1 cup white onion, chopped

2 cloves garlic, minced

1 tsp. dried basil leaves

1/4 tsp. red pepper, crushed

16 oz. can whole tomatoes

14.5 oz. can beef broth

15 oz. can black beans, undrained

15 oz. can butter beans, undrained

This recipe can be doubled for the 18 or 20 quart Roaster Oven.

Brown the Italian sausage in a large sauté pan for 5 minutes. Place the sausage in the cooking pan and add the onion, garlic, basil, red pepper, tomatoes, broth, and beans. Cover and heat the Roaster Oven to 250°F. Simmer the soup for 1 hour, stirring often. Serve warm. Serves 2 hungry people.

BUTTERY LEEK POTATO SOUP

8 boiling potatoes, peeled & diced

8 leeks, sliced

5 cups water

1/2 cup butter or margarine

6 Tbsp. flour

3/4 cup milk

1/4 tsp. salt

1/2 tsp. black pepper

A mild-flavored and comforting soup. Add seasoned croutons on top for a special touch.

Combine the potatoes and leeks with the water in the cooking pan. Cover and cook at 375°F until the soup reaches a full boil. Reduce the heat to 250°F and mash the potatoes slightly, leaving many large pieces of potatoes. Add the butter, flour, milk, salt and pepper and stir until well combined. Simmer for 10 minutes, or until the soup is warm and the leeks are translucent. Serve hot or warm. Serves 6.

*This recipe can be doubled for the 18 or 20 quart Roaster Oven.

NAVY BEAN SOUP— ITALIAN STYLE

Basil and tomatoes add the touch of Italy to this soup.

4 cups navy beans, softened and drained (refer to the directions on the package of beans)

1 lb. ham hock, (equal to 2 cups ham) diced

1 medium white onion, chopped

3 stalks celery, chopped

1 cup carrots, peeled and diced

28 oz. can crushed tomatoes

1 tsp. dried basil leaves

1/4 tsp. salt

1/2 tsp. black pepper

*This recipe can be doubled for the 18 or 20 quart Roaster Oven.

Place the beans, ham, onion, celery, carrots, tomatoes, basil, salt and pepper in the cooking pan. Stir gently to combine the ingredients. Cover the Roaster Oven and heat to 250°F. Simmer for 1½-2 hours. Stir occasionally. Serve hot with dark brown bread. Serves 4.

CLASSIC MINESTRONE

1 clove garlic, minced

2 cups white onion, chopped

1 cup celery, chopped

6 oz. can tomato paste

14 oz. can beef broth

5 cups water

2 large carrots, peeled and sliced thinly

1/2 head cabbage, sliced

2 tsp. salt

1/2 tsp. black pepper

15 oz. can kidney beans

10 oz. frozen peas, thawed

10 oz. frozen green beans, thawed

2 cups uncooked small-shaped pasta of your choice

Combine the garlic, onion, celery, tomato paste, broth, water, carrots, cabbage, salt, pepper, beans, peas and green beans in the cooking pan. Stir thoroughly to combine. Cover and heat at 250°F. Simmer the soup for 1 hour. Add the uncooked pasta and simmer for an additional 15 minutes. To serve, ladle into individual bowls and pass around Parmesan cheese as a topping. Serves 6.

Start with this favorite recipe and add a twist with different pasta shapes, any variety of vegetables and your choice of herbs.

*This recipe can be doubled for the 18 or 20 quart Roaster Oven.

CLASSIC AMERICAN CHILI

Make this delicious chili for your next outdoor barbeque dinner.

*This recipe can be doubled for the 18 or 20 quart Roaster Oven.

1/4 lb. pinto or kidney beans, prepared or canned

2-14.5 oz. cans tomatoes, diced

2 lbs. ground beef, browned and drained

1 green pepper, coarsely chopped

1 medium onion, chopped

2 cloves garlic, crushed

3 Tbsp. chili powder

1 tsp. ground black pepper

1 tsp. ground cumin

1 tsp. salt

hot pepper sauce to taste

Lightly coat the cooking pan with nonstick cooking spray. Layer the beans, tomatoes, ground beef, pepper, onion, garlic, chili powder, black pepper, cumin, salt and hot sauce in the cooking pan. Cover and cook at 250°F for 2-3 hours. Stir occasionally while cooking. Serves 8-10.

WHITE CHICKEN CHILI

2 lbs. chicken, boneless and skinless

1 Tbsp. oil (optional)

1 lb. Great Northern white beans, prepared or canned

1 medium white onion, chopped

3 cloves garlic, chopped

2–4 oz. cans green chilies, diced

2 tsp. ground cumin

1 tsp. dried oregano

1 tsp. ground cayenne pepper

1/2 tsp. salt

14.5 oz. can chicken broth

1 cup water

Cut the chicken into 1-inch cubes. In a medium sauté pan, brown the cubes in the oil. In the cooking pan, combine the beans, onion, garlic, chilies, cumin, oregano, pepper, salt, broth and water. Gently fold in the browned chicken. Cover and cook at 250°F for 2-3 hours, stirring occasionally. Serves 8-10.

This is an excellent alternative to traditional chili.

This recipe can be doubled for the 18 or 20 quart Roaster Oven.

HOMESTYLE BEEF STEW

Chock-full of vegetables and beef.

2 lbs. beef stew meat, cut in 1-inch pieces

1/2 cup dry bread crumbs

1 tsp. salt

1/2 tsp. black pepper

1 medium yellow onion, chopped

1/2 lb. baby carrots, rinsed

1 stalk celery, sliced

3 boiling potatoes, peeled and cubed

1 tsp. dried basil

1/3 cup quick cooking tapioca

1 cup fresh crimini mushrooms, thinly sliced

2-10.5 oz. cans tomato soup

1 cup beef broth

2 Tbsp. Worcestershire sauce

This recipe can be doubled for the 18 or 20 quart Roaster Oven.

In a large bowl, toss the stew meat with the bread crumbs, salt and pepper. Place the beef in the cooking pan and add the onion, carrots, celery, potatoes, basil, tapioca, mushrooms, tomato soup, broth and Worcestershire sauce. Stir well to combine. Cover and roast at 250°F for 4-5 hours, or until the meat is moist and the vegetables are tender to the fork. Serves 6.

Chapter 5

MARINADES, SAUCES & STUFFINGS

Marinades and sauces enhance just about any cut of beef, pork and lamb, as well as poultry and seafood. The tenderness that is injected into the meat by a combination of oil, herbs and spices is the hallmark of an excellent roasted turkey or rolled beef roast. Stuffings not only create spectacular flavors for poultry, they make a wonderful side dish to the main entrée.

To properly prepare marinades, sauces and stuffing, we've included a few hints that will help ensure your success:

- The marinades in this chapter can be used with up to 2 pounds of meat, poultry or seafood. If desired, you may cut the marinade ingredients in half or double the recipe to suit your needs.

- Discard marinades after they've been used with any raw food. This helps eliminate the possibility of contamination from harmful bacteria. If you want to use the marinade as a sauce, cook the marinade in a saucepan on medium temperature until it reaches a full boil. Simmer for 15 minutes and serve.

- If you desire to marinate for flavor and not necessarily to tenderize the meat, you may limit the marinating time to between 15 minutes and 2 hours. To properly tenderize the meat you should plan on marinating for at least 6 hours.

- Do not marinate foods for longer than 24 hours. Food texture begins to break down and become mushy when foods are marinated past that time.

- Always make sure your stuffing reaches the proper cooking temperature. A stuffed turkey or chicken will add at least 30-60 minutes of additional cooking time. Use a meat thermometer or temperature fork and follow the Rival® Cooking Time Charts in Chapter 1.

- There are a number of ways to add delicious flavor to turkey and chicken. Try filling the cavity of the poultry with:

  - Halves of lemon and oranges with slices of onions

  - Sprigs of fresh rosemary or bunches of other fresh herbs, such as tarragon or sage

  - Slices of onions and red peppers or scallions

  - Sliced cloves of garlic

  - Apple and pear halves sprinkled in cinnamon and brown sugar

ZESTY LIME MARINADE

1/2 cup fresh lime juice

2 Tbsp. lime peel, grated

1/2 cup extra-virgin olive oil

2 cloves garlic, minced

1/4 cup fresh cilantro, chopped

2 tsp. red pepper flakes

1/4 tsp. salt

1/2 tsp. black pepper

The lime makes a snappy base for this marinade.

In a plastic, resealable bag, combine the juice, lime peel, olive oil, garlic, cilantro, pepper flakes, salt and pepper. Close the bag and mix the marinade ingredients until well blended. Add up to 2 pounds of chicken, beef, fish or shrimp. Reseal the bag and refrigerate for 2 hours or up to 24 hours.

CARIBBEAN JERK MARINADE

The flavor of the Caribbean comes to your table!

1 white onion, chopped

3/4 cup scallions, chopped

1 tsp. dried thyme

1 tsp. brown sugar

1 tsp. ground allspice

1/4 tsp. ground nutmeg

1 tsp. ground black pepper

1 tsp. red pepper flakes

1/4 cup low-sodium soy sauce

1/4 cup vegetable oil

3 Tbsp. Balsamic vinegar

1/4 tsp. bottled hot sauce

Combine all ingredients in a food processor. Using the pulse switch or low speed, mix the marinade until completely blended and smooth. Pour into a plastic, resealable bag and add up to 2 pounds of chicken or beef. (This marinade works well with shrimp, pork and other meats, as well). Seal and refrigerate for 2 hours or up to 24 hours.

GARLIC ROSEMARY MARINADE

1/4 cup fresh rosemary, chopped

5 cloves garlic, chopped

1/2 cup fresh lemon juice

1/2 cup extra-virgin olive oil

1/4 tsp. salt

1/2 tsp. black pepper

A light, fresh marinade. The tang of lemon offsets the garlic and rosemary.

Combine all ingredients in a food processor using the pulse button or the low speed (you may also mix the ingredients by hand in a small bowl). Do not over-process. Visible pieces of rosemary should remain. Pour into a plastic, resealable bag and add up to 2 pounds of lamb, chicken or pork. Seal and refrigerate for 2 hours or up to 24 hours.

SUNSHINE CITRUS MARINADE

Fruity and light.

juice and zest of 1 lemon
juice and zest of 1 orange
1/4 cup soy sauce
2 Tbsp. fresh ginger, chopped
4 cloves garlic, minced
1/4 cup honey

Combine the juice and zest of the orange and lemon with the soy sauce in a resealable plastic bag. Add the ginger, garlic and honey and thoroughly combine. Add up to 2 pounds of pork or chicken. Seal and refrigerate for 2 hours or up to 24 hours.

NEW ORLEANS BOURBON MARINADE

1/2 cup brown sugar

1/2 cup Dijon mustard

1/2 cup bourbon

1/3 cup soy sauce

1 clove garlic, chopped

2 Tbsp. Worcestershire sauce

1 medium white onion, chopped

1/2 tsp. black pepper

Like the city itself, this marinade holds secret, flavorful delights.

In a small bowl, whisk the sugar, mustard, bourbon, and soy sauce. When well-blended, add the garlic, Worcestershire sauce, onion and black pepper. Pour the marinade into a resealable plastic bag and add up to 2 pounds of beef, chicken, pork or shellfish. Seal and refrigerate for 2 hours or up to 24 hours.

SPICY RUM MARINADE

Excellent with seafood!

2 jalapeño peppers, stems and seeds removed

3/4 cup dark rum

1/2 cup lime juice

3/4 cup vegetable oil

1/4 cup fresh cilantro, chopped

4 cloves garlic, minced

1 tsp. red pepper flakes

In a food processor or blender, purée the peppers, rum and lime juice. Add the oil, cilantro, garlic and pepper flakes and pour into a resealable plastic bag. Add up to 2 pounds of shrimp, chicken or beef. Seal and refrigerate for 2 hours or up to 24 hours.

SAVORY STEAK SAUCE MARINADE

1/2 cup bottled steak sauce
1/4 cup brown sugar, packed
juice of 1 lime
1/2 tsp. red pepper
1/2 tsp. garlic powder

Very good on less-tender cuts of beef.

Combine all ingredients in a plastic resealable bag and mix well. Add up to 2 pounds of shrimp, chicken or beef. Seal and refrigerate for 2 hours or up to 24 hours.

ITALIAN BASIL MARINADE

A quick marinade for any roasted meat, or try this with Italian bread.

2/3 cup bottled Italian salad dressing

2 Tbsp. fresh parsley, coarsely chopped

2 Tbsp. dried basil

Combine all ingredients in a resealable plastic bag and mix well. Add up to 2 pounds of beef, chicken, pork or shellfish. Seal and refrigerate for 2 hours or up to 24 hours.

BOLD BLACK PEPPER MARINADE

1/4 cup vegetable oil

1/4 cup soy sauce

1/4 cup lime juice

3 tsp. Worcestershire sauce

1 Tbsp. black pepper, freshly ground

1 white onion, chopped

2 cloves garlic, minced

A solid marinade for barbeque beef or pork

In a large bowl, mix all the ingredients in the order listed. Use as a marinade for up to 3 pounds of beef or pork.

SOUTH OF THE BORDER MARINADE

Hot and spicy! Excellent with beef.

1 cup prepared salsa

1/4 cup fresh cilantro, chopped

1/2 cup fresh lime juice

1 Tbsp. vegetable oil

1 clove garlic, minced

1/4 tsp. ground cumin

1/2 tsp. ground black pepper

In a plastic, resealable bag, combine the salsa, cilantro, lime juice, oil, garlic, cumin and pepper. Mix thoroughly to combine. Add up to 2 pounds of beef, chicken, pork or shellfish. Seal and refrigerate for 2 hours or up to 24 hours.

BEAUTIFUL BROWNING SAUCE

1/2 cup butter or margarine, melted
2 Tbsp. browning sauce (such as Kitchen Bouquet™)
1/2 tsp. salt
1/2 tsp. ground paprika

When the only flavor you want is the delicious taste of turkey, use this sauce for a golden bird.

Combine all ingredients in a small bowl and stir well to mix. Using a pastry brush, cover the turkey completely with the sauce. Roast the turkey according to the Rival® Cooking Time Charts in Chapter 1. During the last 30 minutes of roasting, increase the Roaster Oven temperature to 400°F. Covers a 14-20 lb. turkey.

ZESTY TURKEY SAUCE

This delicious sauce makes a mouthwatering turkey.

1/2 cup orange juice
1/4 cup soy sauce
1/4 cup honey
1/4 cup vegetable oil
4 cloves garlic, crushed

Combine all ingredients in a small bowl, stirring well to mix. Using a pastry brush, cover the turkey with the sauce. Roast the turkey according to the Rival® Cooking Time Charts in Chapter 1. During the last 30 minutes of roasting, increase the Roaster Oven temperature to 400°F. Covers a 14-20 lb. turkey.

TROPICAL ISLAND SAUCE

1 Tbsp. apricot preserves

4 cloves garlic, crushed

2 Tbsp. bottled hot pepper sauce

1 tsp. black pepper

1 tsp. salt

1/4 cup lime juice

1 tsp. lime peel, shredded

1 tsp. soy sauce

Would you like to be on a tropical island? This sauce will take you there.

Combine all ingredients in a small bowl, stirring well to mix. Using a pastry brush, cover the turkey with the sauce. Roast the turkey according to the Rival® Cooking Time Charts in Chapter 1. During the last 30 minutes of roasting, increase the Roaster Oven temperature to 400°F. Covers a 14-20 lb. turkey.

WHITE WINE SAUCE

A dash of cayenne pepper wakes up this sauce!

1/4 cup vegetable oil

1/4 cup dry white wine

1/2 tsp. cayenne pepper

2 Tbsp. soy sauce

1/2 tsp. garlic powder

1/4 tsp. salt

1/2 tsp. black pepper

Combine all ingredients in a small bowl, stirring well to mix. Using a pastry brush, cover the turkey with the sauce. Roast the turkey according to the Rival® Cooking Time Charts in Chapter 1. During the last 30 minutes of roasting, increase the Roaster Oven temperature to 400°F. Covers a 14-20 lb. turkey.

SOUTHERN SAUCE

2 Tbsp. habañero chili hot sauce
1/2 cup bottled Italian dressing
1/4 cup lemon juice
1/4 cup fresh cilantro, chopped

Cilantro adds the finishing touch.

Combine all ingredients in a small bowl, stirring well to mix. Using a pastry brush, cover the turkey with the sauce. Roast the turkey according to the Rival® Cooking Time Charts in Chapter 1. During the last 30 minutes of roasting, increase the Roaster Oven temperature to 400°F. Covers a 14-20 lb. turkey.

ROSEMARY SAUCE

Herbs and spices create a memorable turkey or chicken.

1 Tbsp. vinegar

3 Tbsp. Dijon mustard

2 Tbsp. garlic, minced

2 Tbsp. dried rosemary, chopped

2 Tbsp. extra-virgin olive oil

1/2 cup lemon juice

Combine all ingredients in a small bowl, stirring well to mix. Using a pastry brush, cover the turkey with the sauce. Roast the turkey according to the Rival® Cooking Time Charts in Chapter 1. During the last 30 minutes of roasting, increase the Roaster Oven temperature to 400°F. Covers a 14-20 lb. turkey.

MEDLEY OF FRUIT STUFFING

2 cups dried cranberries

1 cup dried apricot halves

1/2 cup bourbon

3 Bartlett pears, peeled and diced

1/4 cup prunes, pitted and chopped

1 cup raisins

3 large yellow onions, peeled and diced

3 stalks celery, diced

1/2 cup butter or margarine, melted

2 cups walnuts, chopped

1 Tbsp. ground ginger

3 eggs, slightly beaten

1 cup unflavored bread crumbs

This spectacular stuffing will bring your guests to the table in a flash!

Combine the cranberries, apricot halves and bourbon in a large bowl. Cover and marinate overnight or 12 hours. Add the pears, prunes, raisins, onions, celery, butter, walnuts, ginger, eggs and bread crumbs to the fruit and mix thoroughly to combine. Recipe makes enough to stuff a 14-20 lb. turkey.

CORN BREAD STUFFING

A classic southern stuffing.

1/2 cup unsalted butter, melted

2 white onions, finely diced

2 stalks celery, finely sliced

3 3/4 cups yellow cornmeal

1 1/2 cups chicken broth

2 tsp. freshly ground black pepper

1/4 tsp. salt

1/2 tsp. black pepper

Combine all of the ingredients in a large bowl and mix well. Refrigerate for at least 1 hour or up to 6 hours before stuffing the turkey. Stuffs a 14-20 lb. turkey.

APPLE & WALNUT STUFFING

6 oz. pkg. bread stuffing mix, dry
1 cup walnuts, finely chopped
2 red or green apples, peeled, cored and diced
1/2 cup white onions, chopped

The apples and walnuts add crunch and flavor to this savory stuffing.

Prepare the stuffing mix according to package directions. Add the walnuts, apples and onions and mix lightly.

*This stuffing recipe is sufficient for a 10-12 pound turkey. Adjust the recipe based on the size of the turkey.

ELEGANT MUSHROOM STUFFING

A very fragrant and appealing stuffing for turkey.

1 1/2 lbs. button mushrooms, sliced

1/2 cup butter or margarine, melted

1 cup chicken broth

8 cups bread crumbs, dried

1 cup yellow onions, diced

1 cup celery, chopped

1 tsp. poultry seasoning

2 eggs, beaten

1/4 tsp. salt

1/4 tsp. black pepper

*This stuffing recipe is sufficient for a 10-12 pound turkey. Adjust the recipe based on the size of the turkey.

In a large bowl, combine the mushrooms, butter and chicken broth. Add the bread crumbs, onions, celery, poultry seasoning, eggs, salt and pepper. Mix well.

DIJON MUSTARD STUFFING

1 cup butter or margarine, melted

1/3 cup prepared Dijon style mustard

1 cup yellow onions, chopped

1 cup celery, chopped

1 cup walnuts, chopped

1 tsp. poultry seasoning

1/4 tsp. ground black pepper

7 cups bread crumbs, dried

14.5 oz. can chicken broth

In a large bowl combine the butter and mustard. Add the remaining ingredients and stir until the bread crumbs are well coated.

Onions, celery and walnuts are coated with spicy Dijon mustard.

This stuffing recipe is sufficient for a 10-12 pound turkey. Adjust the recipe based on the size of the turkey.

Chapter 6

SAVORY ROASTED POULTRY

One of the best ways to use your Rival® Roaster Oven is to place a whole chicken or turkey in the cooking pan and let your Roaster Oven go to work. Roasted poultry is extremely moist and tender when cooked in the roaster, and with the addition of herbs, spices and stuffing, almost any meal is a banquet.

In this chapter we offer something for everyone—*Tarragon Chicken Linguini* for a weeknight meal, *Chicken Taco Dinner* for the family, *Roasted Gourmet Chicken* for a dinner party and *Classic Italian-Roasted Turkey* for a delicious variation of traditional turkey.

Cooking your chicken or turkey to the proper temperature is very important to avoid harmful bacteria, so we encourage you to use an internal thermometer for accuracy. Chicken and turkey need to be completely cooked, with no pink remaining, so carefully check poultry after the allotted roasting time and determine whether or not it needs additional roasting. Check our Rival® Cooking Time Charts in Chapter 1 for suggested guidelines.

LEMON GARLIC ROASTED CHICKEN

Lightly flavored chicken—wonderful for picnics.

3–4 lbs. whole chicken, neck and giblets removed

3 cloves garlic, minced

1 tsp. salt

2 Tbsp. lemon juice

1/4 tsp. ground black pepper

1/4 cup butter or margarine, softened

Rinse the chicken in cold water and pat dry. Combine the garlic, salt, lemon juice, pepper and butter in a small bowl and mix well. Rub the blend over the skin of the chicken and the meat. Place the roasting rack in the cooking pan. Position the chicken on the roasting rack and cover. Roast at 350°F for 1-1½ hours, or until the chicken is tender and the internal temperature reading is correct. Serves 4.

ROSEMARY CHICKEN

3–4 lbs. whole chicken, neck and giblets removed

2 Tbsp. extra-virgin olive oil

1 Tbsp. fresh rosemary, chopped

3 cloves garlic, minced

1 tsp. salt

1 tsp. black pepper

1/2 cup lemon juice

A dash of lemon and a pinch of herbs flavor this chicken.

Rinse the chicken in cold water and pat dry. Combine the oil, rosemary, garlic, salt, pepper and lemon juice in a small bowl and mix well. Rub the seasoning blend over the skin of the chicken and the meat. Place the roasting rack in the cooking pan. Position the chicken on the roasting rack and cover. Roast at 350°F for 1-1½ hours, or until the chicken is tender and the internal temperature reading is correct. Serves 4.

EAST INDIAN CURRIED CHICKEN

Adjust the amount of curry powder used, according to your preference.

3-4 lbs. whole chicken, neck and giblets removed

1 tsp. salt

2 Tbsp. curry powder

1/2 cup vegetable oil

3 medium white onions, sliced thinly

4 baking apples, peeled, cored and thinly sliced

Rinse the chicken in cold water and pat dry. Combine the salt, curry powder and vegetable oil in a small bowl and mix well. Rub the blend over the skin of the chicken and the meat. Place the onions and apples in the cavity of the chicken. Position the roasting rack in the cooking pan. Place the chicken on the roasting rack and cover. Roast at 350°F for 1-1½ hours, or until the chicken is tender and the internal temperature reading is correct. Serves 4.

RESTAURANT-STYLE HONEY CHICKEN

3 whole, boneless chicken breasts

2 cups canned chicken broth

1/2 cup honey

1/4 cup lemon juice

1/4 cup vegetable oil

2/3 cup prepared Dijon mustard

3 Tbsp. dark brown sugar

Better than your favorite restaurant chicken!

Preheat the Roaster Oven to 350°F. Rinse the chicken in cold water. Pat dry with paper towels. Combine the broth, honey, lemon juice, oil, mustard and brown sugar in a bowl and add the chicken breasts. Turn the breasts to coat thoroughly. Place the chicken in the cooking pan and add any remaining sauce (*note: if using an 18 or 20 quart Roaster Oven place the chicken in a baking dish, then place into the cooking pan). Roast for 25-40 minutes, or until the chicken breasts are tender and the internal temperature is correct. Serves 8.

CHINESE CHICKEN

Save any leftover chicken for chow mein.

2 1/2 lbs. boneless, skinless chicken breasts

1 tsp. soy sauce

3/4 cup ketchup

3/4 cup water

2 Tbsp. vinegar

1/2 cup brown sugar, packed

1 small yellow onion, diced

1 tsp. garlic powder

Preheat the Roaster Oven to 350°F. Lightly coat the cooking pan with cooking oil. In a medium bowl, mix the soy sauce, ketchup, water, vinegar, brown sugar, yellow onion and garlic powder. Mix well to combine. Place the chicken in the bottom of the cooking pan and pour the sauce over the chicken. Roast for 45-60 minutes, or until the chicken is tender and the internal temperature is correct. Serves 4-6.

BRAISED CHICKEN & VEGETABLES

1/4 cup vegetable oil

3 cloves garlic, minced

3 carrots, thinly sliced

2 yellow onions, thinly sliced

1 lb. sweet potatoes, peeled and sliced

1 cup sun-dried tomato halves, chopped

2/3 cup boiling water

4 bone-in chicken breast halves

2 Tbsp. fresh rosemary, chopped

1 tsp. ground paprika

Sun-dried tomatoes add the finishing touch to these tender chicken breasts.

Preheat the Roaster Oven to 400°F. In a large bowl, combine the oil with all of the vegetables except the sun-dried tomato halves. Coat the vegetables evenly with the oil. Place the vegetables in the Roaster Oven. Cover and roast for 20 minutes. While the vegetables are cooking combine the sun-dried tomatoes with the boiling water and let stand for 10 minutes. Sprinkle the chicken with the rosemary and paprika and place the chicken on top of the vegetables. Add the sun dried tomatoes and water. Cover and cook for an additional 40-50 minutes, or until the internal temperature of the chicken is correct. Serves 4.

ROASTED GOURMET CHICKEN

The artichokes and mushrooms add a continental flair to this chicken. Perfect for guests.

8 chicken breast halves, skinless & boneless

2 Tbsp. butter or margarine

12 oz. marinated artichoke hearts, drained

4.5 oz. canned whole mushrooms, drained

1 cup white onion, chopped

1 1/2 tsp. dried rosemary

1 tsp. salt

1/4 tsp. black pepper

2 cups chicken broth

Preheat the Roaster Oven to 350°F. In a skillet over medium heat, lightly brown the chicken breasts in the butter. Combine the artichokes, mushrooms, onion, rosemary, salt, pepper and chicken broth in a bowl and gently mix together. Place the browned chicken breasts in the bottom of the cooking pan. Arrange the artichoke sauce and seasonings on top of the chicken. Roast for 45-60 minutes, or until the chicken is tender and the internal temperature is correct. Serves 8.

JAMAICAN JERK CHICKEN

1/2 cup cider vinegar

1/4 cup lemon juice

1/4 cup vegetable oil

3 cloves garlic, coarsely chopped

4 jalapeno peppers, seeded and chopped

2 tsp. ground ginger

2 Tbsp. ground allspice

2 Tbsp. ground thyme

2 Tbsp. ground cinnamon

2 Tbsp. sugar

1 tsp. ground black pepper

1 tsp. salt

1 tsp. cayenne pepper

3-4 lbs. chicken, cut into pieces

Excellent flavor in every bite!

In a large bowl, combine the vinegar, lemon juice, oil, garlic, peppers, ginger, allspice, thyme, cinnamon, sugar, pepper, salt and cayenne pepper. Mix well to blend. Add the chicken pieces to the marinade, cover tightly and refrigerate overnight. Place the chicken pieces in the cooking pan and discard the marinade. Cover and roast at 350°F for 45-50 minutes. Serves 4-6.

ALMOND CHICKEN CASSEROLE

A creamy sauce and almonds partner with chicken and rice.

5 cups chicken, cooked and cubed

1/2 cup mayonnaise

1/2 cup plain, unflavored yogurt

10.75 oz. can cream of celery soup

2 cups chicken broth

1 tsp. white pepper

1/2 tsp. salt

3 Tbsp. lemon juice

1 white onion, chopped

1 1/2 cups converted rice

2 cups almonds, sliced and blanched

1 1/2 cups celery

1 cup butter or margarine

2 1/2 cups bread crumbs, seasoned

Preheat the Roaster Oven to 350°F. Lightly spray a 9" x 13" baking dish with cooking spray. In a large bowl, mix together the chicken, mayonnaise, yogurt, soup, broth, pepper, salt, lemon juice, onion, rice, almonds and celery. Spread the mixture evenly in the baking dish. In a small bowl, mix the butter and bread crumbs together. Sprinkle the bread crumb mixture over the top of the chicken. Place the baking dish on the roasting rack in the cooking pan. Cover and cook for 20-35 minutes, or until heated through. Serves 8-10.

APPLE WINE ROASTED CHICKEN

10 pieces chicken

1/4 tsp. salt

1/2 tsp. black pepper

1/2 cup all-purpose flour

1/4 cup vegetable oil, divided

3 cloves garlic, minced

2 white onions, sliced

2 cups fresh mushrooms, sliced

4 each, fresh pears and apples, peeled, quartered, rinsed in lemon water

1 1/2 cups apple wine

The fruit and chicken roast deliciously in the wine!

*This recipe can be doubled for the 18 or 20 quart Roaster Oven.

Rinse the chicken in cold water. Pat dry with paper towels. Place the chicken in a plastic bag and mix with the salt and pepper. Add the flour and shake to thoroughly dust each piece of chicken. In a large sauté pan, brown the chicken pieces in 2 tablespoons of oil. Remove the chicken and place in the cooking pan. In the same sauté pan, cook the garlic and onions in the remaining oil until the onions are soft and translucent. Place the onion mixture and mushrooms in the cooking pan with the chicken and add the pears and apples to the pan. Pour the apple wine over all. Cover and cook at 350°F for 30 minutes, or until the chicken is tender and cooked to the correct internal temperature. Serves 10.

MEDITERRANEAN ROASTED CHICKEN

Olives add the finishing touch to this chicken.

3–4 lbs. whole chicken, neck and giblets removed

2 tsp. salt

1 tsp. black pepper

1/2 cup butter or margarine, melted

1/2 cup fresh parsley, chopped

1/2 cup yellow onion, sliced

1 cup ripe black olives, quartered

This recipe can be doubled for the 18 or 20 quart Roaster Oven.

Rinse the chicken in cold water and pat dry. Combine the salt, pepper, margarine and parsley in a small bowl and mix well. Rub the blend over the skin of the chicken, covering to coat completely. Place the roasting rack in the cooking pan. Place the chicken on the roasting rack and cover with the sliced onion. Cover and bake at 350°F for 1-1½ hours, or until the chicken is tender and cooked to the correct internal temperature. Just before serving, arrange the olives on top. Serves 4.

CHICKEN TACO DINNER

4 lbs. boneless chicken breasts, cubed

1 white onion, chopped

1 green bell pepper, chopped

1.25 oz. taco seasoning mix

2 cups water

2 cups cheddar cheese, shredded

10 packaged taco shells, broken

1 cup sour cream (optional)

1 cup fresh salsa (optional)

1 tomato, chopped

A favorite family meal!

Lightly coat the cooking pan with cooking spray. Layer the chicken breasts, onion and green pepper in the cooking pan. In a medium bowl, combine the taco seasoning mix and water and pour over the chicken breasts and vegetables. Cover and roast at 350°F for 25-30 minutes. Spoon the chicken taco mix onto a large platter. Sprinkle the cheddar cheese and taco shells over the roasted chicken and vegetables. Serve with sour cream, salsa and the chopped tomato. Serves 8.

TARRAGON CHICKEN LINGUINE

You may substitute 2 teaspoons of dried tarragon in place of the fresh tarragon used here. Either way, this is a lovely dish for any special meal.

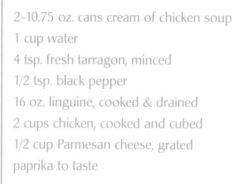

2-10.75 oz. cans cream of chicken soup

1 cup water

4 tsp. fresh tarragon, minced

1/2 tsp. black pepper

16 oz. linguine, cooked & drained

2 cups chicken, cooked and cubed

1/2 cup Parmesan cheese, grated

paprika to taste

In a large bowl, combine the soup, water, tarragon and pepper. Stir in the linguine and chicken. Mix well to combine. Transfer the chicken and pasta to the cooking pan. Cook at 350°F for 25-45 minutes, or until the casserole is completely cooked and hot throughout. Sprinkle with the Parmesan cheese and paprika just prior to serving. Serves 6.

CHEDDAR ONION CHICKEN BAKE

1/2 cup butter or margarine, melted

4 medium onions, sliced

10.75 oz. can cream of celery soup

2 cups cheddar cheese, shredded and divided

2 cups chicken, cooked and cubed

1/4 tsp. salt

1/2 tsp. pepper

Spoon this delightful chicken entrée over pasta or rice.

Place the melted butter in the cooking pan and arrange the onions on top. In a large bowl, combine the soup, 1 cup of the cheese, chicken, salt and pepper. Spoon the chicken and cheese on top of the onions. Roast at 350°F for 30-40 minutes. During the last five minutes of roasting, sprinkle the remaining cheese on top. Serves 4.

This recipe can be doubled for the 18 or 20 quart Roaster Oven. You may also use a 9" x 13" baking pan. Position the baking ban on the roasting rack and heat as directed.

HERB-CRUSTED SWISS CHICKEN

Crunchy herb croutons and melted cheese create this special entrée.

6 boneless, skinless chicken breasts

6 slices Swiss cheese

10.75 oz. can cream of celery soup

1 cup evaporated milk

2 cups herb-seasoned stuffing cubes

1/2 cup butter or margarine, melted

*This recipe can be doubled for the 18 or 20 quart Roaster Oven. You may also use a 9" x 13" baking pan. Position the baking ban on the roasting rack and heat as directed.

Arrange the chicken breasts in the cooking pan and top with the Swiss cheese. Combine the soup and milk and blend well. Spoon the soup over the cheese and chicken. Sprinkle the stuffing mix evenly over the casserole and drizzle the melted butter over the top. Cook at 350°F for 45-55 minutes. Increase the temperature to 400°F and cook for 10 minutes. Serves 6.

CREOLE CHICKEN & SHRIMP

1 cup instant rice, uncooked

2 cups chicken broth

1 Tbsp. red pepper sauce

1 medium onion, chopped

1 clove garlic, crushed

2 cups cut-up chicken, cooked

1 cup smoked ham, fully cooked & finely chopped

1/4 cup tomato paste

1 small green bell pepper, chopped

16 oz. can whole tomatoes, undrained

6.5 oz. frozen shrimp, rinsed and drained

Preheat the Roaster Oven to 350°F. In a large bowl, mix together the rice, broth, pepper sauce, onion and garlic. Stir in the remaining ingredients. Gently break up the tomatoes as you stir the casserole. Pour the casserole into the cooking pan. Cook for 40 minutes or until all of the liquid is absorbed and the casserole is thoroughly hot. Serves 6.

Louisiana flavor in every bite!

This recipe can be doubled for the 18 or 20 quart Roaster Oven.

ROASTED BBQ CHICKEN

Chili powder seasons the entire sauce with that "outdoors" flavor.

*This recipe can be doubled for the 18 or 20 quart Roaster Oven.

1 cup all purpose flour

2 tsp. salt

3 lbs. boneless, skinless chicken breasts

1/2 cup extra-virgin olive oil

1 white onion, diced

1/2 cup celery, diced

1 green bell pepper, diced

1 cup ketchup

1 Tbsp. salt

1 Tbsp. dried basil

1 Tbsp. chili powder

1/3 tsp. black pepper

In a large bowl, mix the flour and 2 tsp. of salt. Heat the oil in a sauté pan over medium heat. Dredge the chicken in the spiced flour and place each breast in the sauté pan. Brown the chicken on both sides. In a small bowl, mix the onion, celery, green pepper, ketchup, salt, dried basil, chili powder and pepper. Place the chicken in the cooking pan and pour the sauce on top. Cover and cook for 35-40 minutes, or until chicken is completely cooked and the internal temperature is correct. Serves 4-6.

PROVENÇAL CHICKEN

3–4 lbs. roasting chicken, cut into pieces

4 Tbsp. olive oil, divided

1 lb. eggplant, diced

2 large yellow onions, diced

3 Tbsp. garlic, minced

2 Tbsp. dried marjoram, crumbled

1 1/2 cups cherry tomatoes, halved

1 cup ripe olive halves, pitted

1 cup chicken broth

A taste of France!

In a large sauté pan, heat 1 tablespoon of oil and add the chicken pieces. Brown the chicken pieces on all sides over moderately high heat. Drain the chicken on paper towels. In a medium bowl, combine the eggplant, onions, garlic, marjoram, tomatoes and olives and mix well. Place the chicken in the cooking pan and evenly spread the vegetables and seasonings over the chicken. Pour the chicken broth over all. Cover and cook at 350°F for 1-1¼ hours, or until the chicken is completely cooked and the internal temperature is correct. Serves 6.

CHICKEN TETRAZZINI

An all-American classic for any potluck dinner.

8 oz. spaghetti, broken and cooked (according to package directions)

5 cups chicken, cooked and cut into cubes

1 red bell pepper, chopped

1 cup chicken broth

1 cup yellow onions, chopped

2-10.5 oz. cans cream of mushroom soup

1 lb. mozzarella cheese, shredded

1 tsp. pepper

1/4 tsp. salt

This recipe can be doubled for the 18 quart or 20 quart Roaster Oven.

Combine all of the ingredients in the cooking pan. Cover and cook at 350°F for 15-25 minutes, or until heated through. Serves 8.

GREEK STUFFED CHICKEN BREASTS

10 cloves garlic, diced

1/4 cup bread crumbs, seasoned

1/4 cup lemon juice

1/3 cup fresh parsley, chopped

1/4 cup feta cheese

1/4 cup Greek olives, chopped

4 bone-in chicken breasts

A flavorful pocket of cheese and herbs enhances each chicken breast.

Preheat the Roaster Oven to 350°F. In a small bowl, combine the garlic, bread crumbs, lemon juice, parsley, feta cheese and olives. With a sharp knife, cut a 2-inch long pocket, 2-inches deep along the breast bone side of the chicken, without cutting all the way through. Spoon the stuffing evenly into the pockets. Place the chicken breasts on the roasting rack in the cooking pan. Cover and cook for 25-35 minutes or until the internal cooking temperature is correct. Serves 4.

*This recipe can be doubled for the 18 or 20 quart Roaster Oven.

SPICY KOREAN CHICKEN

If you like spicy, add additional pepper flakes until the heat factor is just right for you!

4 chicken breast halves

2 Tbsp. sesame oil

3/4 cup soy sauce

1/4 cup lime juice

2 Tbsp. brown sugar

1/2 tsp. red pepper flakes, crushed

1 tsp. ginger, powdered

*Use a small loaf pan and decrease the recipe by half when using the 6, 8 or 10 quart Roaster Oven.

Preheat the Roaster Oven to 350°F. Place the chicken, skin side facing up, in a 9" x 13" baking dish. In a bowl, whisk the oil, soy sauce, lime juice, sugar, red pepper flakes and ginger. Pour the marinade over the chicken. Place the baking dish on the roasting rack in the cooking pan. Cover and cook for 50-60 minutes at 350°F.

GOLDEN HOLIDAY TURKEY

14–20 lbs. turkey, neck and giblets removed

1/4 cup vegetable oil

1/4 cup dry white wine

1/2 tsp. cayenne pepper

2 Tbsp. soy sauce

1/2 tsp. garlic powder

salt and pepper to taste

Perfect for the holidays or any time the entire family dines together.

Thoroughly clean the turkey and pat dry. Stir the oil, wine, pepper, soy sauce, garlic powder, salt and pepper together in a small bowl. Place the turkey on the roasting rack in the cooking pan. Using a pastry brush, cover the turkey completely with the sauce. Roast according to the Rival® Cooking Time Charts in Chapter 1. During the last 30 minutes of roasting, increase the oven temperature to 400°F. Serves 12-16.

CLASSIC ITALIAN ROASTED TURKEY

A simple sauce adorns this delicious turkey.

14-20 lbs. turkey, neck and giblets removed

1/4 cup extra virgin olive oil

1/2 cup balsamic vinegar

2 Tbsp. fresh garlic, chopped

Thoroughly clean the turkey and pat dry. Stir the oil, vinegar and garlic together in a small bowl. Place the turkey on the roasting rack in the cooking pan. Using a pastry brush, cover the turkey completely with the sauce. Roast according to the Rival® Cooking Time Charts in Chapter 1. During the last 30 minutes of roasting, increase the oven temperature to 400°F. Serves 12-16.

CREAMY SWISS TURKEY BAKE

5 leeks, sliced

3 Tbsp. butter

1/2 tsp. salt

1/4 tsp. ground nutmeg

1/8 tsp. black pepper

1 cup chicken broth

10.75 oz. can cream of celery soup

1 cup water

1 cup celery, chopped

3 cups cooked turkey, cubed

1/2 cup smoked ham, chopped

3 cups hot pasta noodles, cooked

1 cup Swiss cheese, shredded

Over medium heat in a large sauté pan, cook the leeks in the butter for 5 minutes. Stir in the salt, nutmeg and pepper. Remove from the heat and blend in the chicken broth, soup and water, mixing well. Return to the stove and heat to boiling, stirring constantly. Add the celery, turkey and ham and mix again. Toss the noodles into the turkey casserole and spread evenly in the cooking pan. Sprinkle the cheese over the casserole. Cook at 350°F for 25-30 minutes. Serves 8.

A lovely entrée complete with ham, turkey, leeks and Swiss cheese.

This recipe can be doubled for the 18 or 20 quart Roaster Oven.

107

Chapter 7

TENDER ROASTED BEEF RECIPES

Roasting is the perfect cooking method for beef. Not only does roasting lock in the flavor and natural juices of the beef, it tenderizes meats while cooking because liquids do not evaporate as they would in a conventional oven. What's the result? Perfectly moist and tender beef every time!

When choosing beef for your meal, it's best to remove the visible fat. Use less tender and less expensive cuts of beef for family-style dining. Try *Smooth Whiskey Roast,* using a round roast, or *Hearty American Pot Roast with Vegetables,* using a chuck roast. When you are preparing an elegant meal you'll find that *Bourbon Rib Eye Roast* and *Southern Roast Beef* are good choices with tender and especially flavorful cuts of beef.

Beef is best when cooked to your preference, so we offer general guidelines in our Rival® Cooking Time and Temperature Charts in Chapter 1. It's best to underestimate the cooking time, rather than overestimate, so start with the lowest amount of time that may be required and check from that point on. Use an internal meat thermometer for accuracy whenever testing beef.

TENDER SWEET ROAST

Nothing melts in your mouth like a piece of tender roast. Serve with potatoes and gravy.

1 Tbsp. butter or margarine

4 lbs. beef rump roast

4 anchovies, chopped

1 white onion, minced

2 tsp. salt

15 peppercorns

1 Tbsp. brown sugar

1 Tbsp. apple cider vinegar

1 Tbsp. whiskey

1 cup water

*This recipe can be doubled for the 18 or 20 quart Roaster Oven, but increase the cooking time based on 12-20 minutes per pound of beef roasting at 325°F.

Preheat the Roaster Oven to 325°F. Place the butter in the cooking pan and stir to melt. Add the beef, anchovies, onion, salt, peppercorns, sugar, vinegar, whiskey and water. Cover and cook for 48-60 minutes, or until the roast is tender and cooked to your preference. Serves 10.

110

GARLIC ROAST BEEF

4 lbs. beef roast

2 Tbsp. olive oil

3 cloves garlic, peeled and crushed

1 cup bread crumbs

1/2 cup fresh parsley, chopped

1/2 cup fresh basil, chopped

1/2 tsp. salt

1/2 tsp. black pepper

Saturated with garlic and herbs, this roast offers rich flavors in every bite.

Pat the roast with paper towels until dry and place it on the roasting rack in the cooking pan. In a medium bowl, combine the oil, garlic, bread crumbs, parsley, basil, salt and pepper and toss to combine. Sprinkle the garlic/herb mixture on top of the roast. Cover and roast at 325°F for 48-60 minutes, or until the roast is tender and cooked to your preference. Serves 10.

*This recipe can be doubled for the 18 or 20 quart Roaster Oven, but increase the cooking time based on 12-20 minutes per pound of beef roasting at 325°F.

SOUTHERN ROAST BEEF

Serve this tasty roast with pan-fried potatoes and a fresh green salad as accompaniments.

1 cup yellow onion, chopped

1 tsp. black pepper

1 cup celery, chopped very fine

1 Tbsp. garlic, minced

1 cup green bell pepper, chopped fine

1 tsp. dry mustard

1/2 tsp. ground cumin

2 Tbsp. butter, unsalted

1/2 tsp. ground cayenne pepper

1 tsp. salt

1 tsp. white pepper

4 lbs. boneless sirloin roast

This recipe can be doubled for the 18 or 20 quart Roaster Oven, but increase the cooking time based on 12-20 minutes per pound of beef roasting at 325°F.

Preheat the Roaster Oven to 325°F. In a small bowl, combine the onion, pepper, celery, garlic, green pepper, mustard, cumin, butter, cayenne pepper, salt and white pepper. Using a sharp knife, make cuts 1/2-inch in depth over the entire roast. Coat the roast thoroughly with the vegetables and seasonings, patting as much as possible onto the roast. Place the roast on the roasting rack in the cooking pan. Sprinkle any excess seasoning over the top of the roast. Cover and roast for 48-60 minutes, or until the roast is tender and cooked to your preference. Serves 10.

BOURBON RIB EYE ROAST

1/2 cup vegetable oil

1/2 cup bourbon

1 large yellow onion, thinly sliced

2 large cloves garlic, minced

1 tsp. freshly ground black pepper

1/2 tsp. ground cumin

1 tsp. salt

1/4 cup wine or cider vinegar

4 lbs. rib eye roast

Hearty flavors for a tender cut of beef!

In a resealable plastic bag, combine the oil, bourbon, onion, garlic, pepper, cumin, salt and wine or vinegar, blending well. Place the meat in the plastic bag and thoroughly combine with the marinade. Seal and refrigerate for at least 1 hour or up to 24 hours. Place the rib eye on the roasting rack in the cooking pan. Pour any excess marinade over the top of the roast. Cover and roast for 48-60 minutes at 325°F, or until the roast is tender and cooked to your preference. Serves 10.

*This recipe can be doubled for the 18 quart or 20 quart Roaster Oven, but increase the cooking time based on 12-20 minutes per pound of beef roasting at 325°F.

SMOOTH WHISKEY ROAST

Deep flavors in each bite make this a delicious entrée for you and your guests. Serve with wild rice and mushrooms.

1 cup premium whiskey

3/4 cup brown sugar

1/4 cup soy sauce

1 cup water

2 Tbsp. Worcestershire sauce

1 Tbsp. lemon juice

1 tsp. garlic powder

4 lbs. top round roast

*This recipe can be doubled for the 18 or 20 quart Roaster Oven, but increase the cooking time based on 12-20 minutes per pound of beef roasting at 325°F.

In a resealable plastic bag, combine the whiskey, brown sugar, soy sauce, water, Worcestershire sauce, lemon juice and garlic powder, mixing well. Place the roast in the bag, seal, and refrigerate for 12 hours or overnight, turning occasionally. Place the roast on the roasting rack in the cooking pan. Pour any excess marinade over the top of the roast. Cover and roast for 48-60 minutes at 325°F, or until the roast is tender and cooked to your preference. Serves 10.

HICKORY SMOKED BRISKET

4 lbs. beef brisket
1/4 cup bottled liquid smoke
1/2 tsp. garlic salt
1/2 tsp. onion powder
1/2 tsp. celery salt

All the flavor of barbeque with none of the work!

Place the brisket on a large piece of aluminum foil. Generously sprinkle with the liquid smoke and seasonings. Wrap the brisket in the foil and crimp the edges to seal. Place in the cooking pan. Cover and roast at 250°F for 4 hours. Serves 10.

*This recipe can be doubled for the 18 or 20 quart Roaster Oven, but increase the cooking time based on 12-20 minutes per pound of beef roasting at 250°F.

115

HEARTY AMERICAN POT ROAST WITH VEGETABLES

Perfect for the first cold evening of winter.

3-4 lbs. beef chuck roast

1 cup baby carrots

4 medium baking potatoes, peeled & quartered

1 white onion, quartered

2 tsp. salt

1/2 tsp. black pepper

1 cup beef broth

*This recipe can be doubled for the 18 or 20 quart Roaster Oven, but increase the cooking time based on 12-20 minutes per pound of beef roasting at 250°F.

Place the roast in the bottom of the cooking pan. Arrange the carrots, potatoes and onion around the sides of roast. Add the salt, pepper and broth. Cover and roast at 250°F for 3-4 hours or until tender and cooked to your preference. Serves 6.

SPICY HERBED BEEF

4 lbs. round roast

1/4 cup vinegar

2 Tbsp. Worcestershire sauce

2 Tbsp. garlic, minced

1 Tbsp. dried oregano

1 small onion, diced

.7 oz. pkg. Italian dressing mix

2 tsp. dried basil

1/4 tsp. salt

1/2 tsp. black pepper

Oregano and basil bring out the best flavors of this roast. Delicious hot or cold in deli-style sandwiches.

Using a sharp knife, make cuts ½-inch deep over the entire roast. In a small bowl, whisk together the vinegar, Worcestershire sauce, garlic, oregano, onion, dressing mix, basil, salt and pepper. Place the roast on the roasting rack in the cooking pan. Spoon the sauce over the roast. Cover and roast at 325°F for 48-60 minutes, or until tender and cooked to your preference. Serves 10.

*This recipe can be doubled for the 18 or 20 quart Roaster Oven, but increase the cooking time based on 12-20 minutes per pound of beef roasting at 325°F.

117

BEEF, BROCCOLI & RICE BOWL

This is a perfect entrée for your next neighborhood potluck dinner.

2–10.75 oz. cans cream of broccoli soup

2 cups water

2 lbs. ground beef, browned

10 oz. frozen, chopped broccoli, thawed and drained

1 cup yellow onion, chopped

4 oz. processed cheese, chopped

1 clove garlic, minced

1 cup converted rice

1/4 tsp. salt

1/2 tsp. black pepper

*This recipe can be doubled for the 18 or 20 quart Roaster Oven, or you may use a 9" x 13" baking pan inside the Roaster Oven. If using a baking pan, be sure to coat the pan with cooking spray and use the roasting rack.

In a large bowl, combine the soup and water. Fold into the soup the browned ground beef, broccoli, onion, cheese, garlic, rice, salt and pepper. Mix well to combine. Pour the casserole into the cooking pan. Bake at 350°F for 45-60 minutes, or until completely cooked and hot. Serves 10.

EASY ROAST BEEF DINNER

5 lbs. top round beef

1/2 cup butter or margarine, melted

1/4 cup sugar

1/4 cup brown sugar, packed

3 lbs. baking potatoes, peeled and diced

1 lb. carrots, peeled and diced

2-0.75 oz. pkgs. dry gravy mix

2 cups water

A very easy way to satisfy hearty appetites!

Lightly coat the cooking pan with nonstick cooking spray. Cover the beef with the melted butter and sprinkle with the sugars; set aside. Arrange the potatoes and carrots in the bottom of the cooking pan. Sprinkle one package of gravy mix over the vegetables. Place the beef on top of the vegetables in the center of the pan. Sprinkle the remaining gravy package over the roast. Add the 2 cups of water to the cooking pan. Cover and roast at 325°F for 2-2½ hours, or until cooked to your preference. Serves 8.

SPICY ITALIAN MEATBALLS WITH HOMEMADE MARINARA SAUCE

A wonderful bite of Italy!

Marinara Sauce

3 cups tomato juice

2–28 oz. cans tomatoes, diced

6 oz. tomato paste

3 cups water

2 cloves garlic, minced

1/4 cup basil leaves, chopped

2 Tbsp. dried oregano

1 Tbsp. dried parsley

1 tsp. salt

1 tsp. pepper

Preheat the Roaster Oven to 350°F. Combine all of the ingredients in the cooking pan and mix thoroughly. Cover and cook for 2 hours. Add the prepared meatballs (recipe follows) and cook for 1 additional hour. While cooking, stir occasionally to ensure even cooking. Serves 6-8.

Meatballs:

2 1/2 lbs. ground beef

1/2 cup bread crumbs, seasoned

2 eggs

1/2 tsp. black pepper

Combine the beef, bread crumbs, eggs and pepper in a large bowl; mix well. Form the beef into 1-inch balls. Place the meatballs in the cooking pan with the Marinara Sauce and turn to coat. Cook as directed above.

Chapter 8

HEARTY ROASTED PORK, HAM & LAMB

Pork is a surprisingly mellow and easy meat to roast. The lean cuts of pork adapt well to the moist roasting methods of the Rival® Roaster Oven and we've included several recipes that add sauces or marinades for extra flavor. Equally easy to roast are the more rich cuts of pork, including the shoulder roasts, chops and spareribs. For special occasions, try *Honey-Orange Pork Tenderloin* or *BBQ Pork Steaks* and for days when you want to prepare dinner early and have it ready when you are try *Quick & Easy Pork Roast* or *Pork with Horseradish Mustard Sauce.*

Ham is one of the most flavorful meats because it is smoked for rich taste. We've touched up ham in this chapter by offering some delicious glazes and sauces. Once you try these you'll want to add your own.

Lamb is rich, tender and high in protein. It can carry a high fat content, so you'll want to remove visible fat as much as possible before roasting. For a classic Greek dinner try our *Greek Island Honeyed Lamb,* and for a sophisticated evening choose *Roasted Lamb Shanks in White Wine.* Truly Delightful!

QUICK & EASY PORK ROAST

A tasty garlic and pepper coat covers this pork roast.

4-5 lbs. pork loin roast

4 cloves garlic, chopped

1 tsp. salt

1/2 tsp. black pepper

1/2 cup bottled Italian dressing

1/4 cup Worcestershire sauce

Preheat the Roaster Oven to 350°F. Place the pork roast on the rack and press the chopped garlic into surface of the roast. Sprinkle the roast with salt and pepper. Place the rack in the cooking pan. Combine the Italian dressing and Worcestershire sauce in a small bowl and brush over the roast. Cover and roast for 2-2½ hours, or until tender and cooked to your preference. Serves 10.

SPICY PINEAPPLE PORK

2 Tbsp. soy sauce

1 Tbsp. fresh ginger, minced

1 clove garlic, minced

4 pork chops, 1-inch thick (about 2 lbs.)

2 Tbsp. chicken broth

1 1/4 cups cider vinegar

3 Tbsp. brown sugar

2 Tbsp. cornstarch

1 Tbsp. red chili peppers, crushed

1 1/4 cups fresh pineapple, diced

1/2 cup cashews, chopped or whole

Combine the soy sauce, ginger and garlic in a plastic resealable bag. Marinate the pork in the sauce for 1 hour in the refrigerator. Combine the broth, vinegar, brown sugar, cornstarch and chili peppers. Place the pork chops in the cooking pan and discard the marinade. Pour the broth & vinegar sauce over the chops and add the pineapple and cashews. Cover and roast at 325°F for 30-40 minutes, or until tender and cooked to your preference. Serves 4.

Serve with steamed rice and tropical fruit.

This recipe can be doubled for the 18 or 20 quart Roaster Oven.

HONEY-ORANGE PORK TENDERLOIN

Orange juice is the tenderizing ingredient in this recipe. It's flavor is prominent and adds a touch of zest to the meat.

4 lbs. pork loin

1 cup chicken broth

1/2 cup honey

1/2 cup soy sauce

1 Tbsp. cornstarch

1 Tbsp. ground ginger

3 cloves garlic, minced

1 cup orange juice

2 Tbsp. sesame seeds

1/2 cup dry sherry

Use a sharp knife to make slices ½-inch in depth over the entire pork loin. Combine the broth, honey, soy sauce, cornstarch, ginger, garlic, orange juice, sesame seeds and sherry in a resealable plastic bag and mix well. Add the pork and refrigerate for at least 1 hour or up to 24 hours. When ready to roast, preheat the Roaster Oven to 350°F. Place the pork loin on the roasting rack in the cooking pan. Pour the remaining marinade over the pork. Cover and roast for 1½-2 hours, or until tender and cooked to your preference. Allow the pork loin to cool for 15 minutes before slicing. Serves 8-10.

ROSEMARY PORK ROAST

2 Tbsp. olive oil

3 Tbsp. garlic, minced

3 Tbsp. dried rosemary

1 tsp. sea salt (or regular salt)

1 tsp. ground pepper

3 lbs. pork tenderloin

Rosemary & garlic infuse this pork tenderloin with delectable flavors.

In a small bowl combine the oil, garlic, rosemary, salt and pepper and mix well. Place the pork in the bottom of the cooking pan on the roasting rack. Pour the sauce over the pork. Cover and roast at 350°F for 1-1½ hours, or until the internal temperature is correct.

SMOKED ROAST PORK

Perfect for your next large family gathering!

4 lbs. pork shoulder roast

1/2 cup soy sauce

1 tsp. garlic powder

1 tsp. ground ginger

1 1/2 tsp. bottled liquid smoke seasoning

*This recipe can be doubled for the 18 or 20 quart Roaster Oven.

Combine all ingredients in a large resealable plastic bag and refrigerate overnight. Preheat the Roaster Oven to 350°F. Place the pork roast on the roasting rack in the cooking pan. Pour the remaining marinade over the pork. Cover and roast for 1½-2 hours, or until tender and cooked to your preference. Allow the pork roast to cool for 15 minutes before slicing. Serves 8-10.

PORK WITH HORSERADISH MUSTARD RUB

3-4 lbs. boneless pork loin roast

2 tsp. olive or vegetable oil

3 tsp. ground dry mustard

1 tsp. garlic powder

1 tsp. ground ginger

1 cup horseradish mustard

Adds a delicious kick to mild-flavored pork.

This recipe can be doubled for the 18 or 20 quart Roaster Oven.

Rub the roast with oil. Combine the mustard, garlic powder, ginger and horseradish mustard and coat the roast thoroughly. Place the roast in a large resealable plastic bag in the refrigerator. Marinate for at least 1 hour or up to 24 hours. Preheat the Roaster Oven to 350°F. Place the pork loin on the roasting rack and place in the cooking pan. Cover and roast for 1½-2 hours, or until tender and cooked to your preference. Allow the pork loin to cool for 15 minutes before slicing. Serves 8-10.

BBQ PORK STEAKS

Melt-in-your-mouth great flavor!

4 pork blade steaks

1 cup bottled barbecue sauce

1/3 cup honey

1 Tbsp. Worcestershire sauce

1 tsp. garlic salt

1 tsp. black pepper

1/2 tsp. prepared mustard

In a small bowl, combine the barbecue sauce, honey, Worcestershire sauce, garlic salt, pepper and mustard. Mix well to blend. Preheat the Roaster Oven to 350°F and brush both sides of each pork steak with the sauce. Place the steaks in the bottom of the cooking pan, cover and roast for 30-45 minutes. Turn the steaks once during cooking. Serves 4.

DRIZZLED PORK CHOPS & SWEET POTATOES

1 Tbsp. vegetable oil

4 pork chops, 1/2-inch thick

2 sweet potatoes, peeled and chopped

1 medium white onion, chopped

2 cups orange juice

4 whole cloves

1/2 Tbsp. salt

1/4 tsp. bottled hot sauce

1 Tbsp. white wine vinegar

1 Tbsp. cornstarch

2 Tbsp. fresh parsley, chopped

A spice-filled sauce with a hint of "heat" roasts with the pork chops.

In a large skillet, heat the oil and brown the pork chops on both sides. Arrange the potatoes and onion in the bottom of the cooking pan and place the pork chops on top of the onions. In a medium bowl, combine the orange juice, cloves, salt, hot sauce, vinegar and cornstarch. Pour the sauce over the pork chops and sprinkle with the parsley. Cook at 350°F for 45-60 minutes. Serves 4.

SWEET & SOUR PORK

This traditional dish is easy to prepare and delicious to eat! Serve over steamed rice.

1/2 cup cider vinegar

2/3 cup pineapple juice

1/2 cup ketchup

2 Tbsp. soy sauce

3 Tbsp. brown sugar

1/4 cup sugar

2 lbs. pork, cubed and browned

1 green pepper, roughly chopped

20 oz. can pineapple chunks, drained

1 Tbsp. cornstarch

1 Tbsp. water

Lightly coat the cooking pan with cooking spray. Combine and stir the vinegar, pineapple juice, ketchup, soy sauce, brown sugar and sugar in the cooking pan. When well blended, add the pork. Cover and cook at 300°F for 20-30 minutes. Add the green pepper and pineapple chunks. In a small bowl, mix the water and cornstarch and stir into the pork & sauce. Cover and continue cooking for 20-35 minutes, or until the sauce is thickened. Serve over hot rice. Serves 4 to 6.

PAPRIKA PORK SPARERIBS & RICE CASSEROLE

1 Tbsp. oil

2 1/2 lbs. pork spareribs

1/4 tsp. salt

1/2 tsp. pepper

1 yellow onion, chopped

4 cloves garlic, chopped

2-14.5 oz. cans beef broth

2 cups converted rice

15.5 oz. can chickpeas, drained

2/3 cup water

1 Tbsp. ground paprika

1 Tbsp. ground oregano

A zesty sauce coats the spareribs, rice and chickpeas.

Preheat the Roaster Oven to 350°F. Lightly grease a 9" x 13" baking dish. Heat the oil in a frying pan over medium heat. Season the spareribs with the salt and pepper and add to the frying pan. Lightly brown the spareribs. Place the ribs in the bottom of the baking dish. Combine all of the remaining ingredients in a large bowl and pour over the spareribs. Place the baking dish on the roasting rack in the cooking pan. Cover and cook for 45-60 minutes, or until the cooking temperature is correct.

133

APRICOT & MUSTARD GLAZED HAM

The preserves give the ham a beautiful glaze.

4 lbs. fully cooked ham

1/2 cup apricot preserves

3 Tbsp. dry mustard

1/2 cup light brown sugar, packed

Preheat the Roaster Oven to 325°F. Score the surface of the ham with shallow diamond-shaped cuts. Combine the preserves and mustard and spread over the ham. Pat brown sugar over the apricot mixture. Place the ham on the roasting rack and place the rack inside the oven on the cooking pan. Roast the ham for 1-1½ hours. Serves 10.

HOLIDAY HONEY HAM

2 cups honey

1/2 cup cider vinegar

2 Tbsp. ground cloves

2 cups brown sugar, packed

2 Tbsp. ground cinnamon

5 lbs. ham, cooked

This ham is easy to prepare and rivals the very expensive brands at the store.

Preheat the Roaster Oven to 275°F. Combine the honey, vinegar, cloves, brown sugar and cinnamon in a small bowl. Place the ham on the roasting rack in the cooking pan. Pour the sauce over the ham. Cover and roast at 275°F for about 1-1½ hours (or more) to heat through completely. Serves 10.

GREEK ISLAND HONEYED LAMB

Sweet-flavored meat with raisins and carrots.

1/2 cup honey

1 cup water

1 cup orange juice

4 lbs. boneless shoulder of lamb

2 large white onions, finely chopped

1 cup raisins

4 carrots, peeled and cut into 1-inch lengths

1 Tbsp. ground cinnamon

1/4 tsp. salt

1/2 tsp. black pepper

2 cups garbanzo beans

*This recipe can be doubled for the 18 or 20 quart Roaster Oven.

In a large bowl, combine the honey, water and orange juice; mix together. Add the lamb, onions, raisins, carrots, cinnamon, salt and pepper. Mix well again. Place the lamb mixture in the bottom of the cooking pan. Cover and roast at 250°F for 4-5 hours. During the last hour of cooking, add the garbanzo beans. Serves 10.

ROASTED LEG OF LAMB

2-5 lbs. semi-boneless leg of lamb, fat trimmed to 1/2-inch thick and tied

5 cloves garlic

1 Tbsp. fine sea salt

3 Tbsp. fresh rosemary, chopped

1/2 tsp. cracked black pepper

1/2 cup fresh lemon juice

3 Tbsp. extra virgin olive oil

4 sprigs of rosemary

Look for sea salt in the specialty spice aisle of your grocery store.

*This recipe can be doubled for the 18 or 20 quart Roaster Oven.

Pound the garlic to a paste. Add the sea salt and pound again. Add the chopped rosemary and pepper. Mix together the fresh lemon juice and olive oil and add to the garlic and seasonings. Rub the sauce completely over the lamb and refrigerate for at least 3 hours or up to 24 hours. Slip the sprigs of rosemary underneath the string of the lamb. Roast at 350°F for 25 minutes per pound, or until the desired cooking temperature is reached. Serves 6.

ROASTED LAMB SHANKS IN WHITE WINE

Sophisticated flavors and easy preparation.

4 large lamb shanks, cracked

4 cloves garlic, minced

1/2 tsp. salt

1 tsp. black pepper

1 medium onion, thinly sliced

1 lb. baby carrots, cut in thin strips

2 stalks celery, cut into 2-inch strips

2 whole bay leaves, crumbled

1 tsp. ground oregano

1 tsp. ground thyme

1/2 cup dry white wine

3 large beefsteak tomatoes, diced

1/4 cup lemon juice

*This recipe can be doubled for the 18 or 20 quart Roaster Oven.

Lightly coat the bottom of the cooking pan with oil or cooking spray. Rub the lamb with garlic and season with salt and pepper. Place the shanks in the bottom of the cooking pan. In a large bowl, combine the onion, carrots, celery, bay leaves, oregano, thyme, wine, tomatoes and lemon juice and stir to mix well. Carefully pour the vegetables and seasonings over the lamb shanks. Cover and roast at 350°F for 1-1½ hours, or until tender and cooked to your preference. Serves 6.

TENDER ROSEMARY LAMB CHOPS

3 cloves garlic, minced

1/3 cup fresh lemon juice

1/2 cup olive oil

1/4 cup fresh rosemary, chopped

4 lamb shoulder chops

The lamb is basted with juices during roasting, creating a succulent chop.

This recipe can be doubled for the 18 or 20 quart Roaster Oven.

In a medium bowl, combine the garlic, lemon juice, olive oil and rosemary and whisk well. Place the lamb in a baking pan and pour the marinade over the lamb, turning to coat all sides. Allow the lamb to marinate in the refrigerator for at least 1 hour or up to 24 hours. Place the lamb on the roasting rack in the cooking pan. Cover and roast at 350°F for 35-50 minutes, or until tender and cooked to your preference. During roasting, baste the lamb with the juices in the bottom of the pan. Serves 4.

JALAPEÑO-PEPPERED LAMB

The peppers add heat and the vegetables add mild flavor to this lamb entrée.

4 lbs. boneless lamb

5 jalapeño peppers, stems removed and chopped

1 green bell pepper, chopped

1/4 cup vegetable oil

2 medium white onions, chopped

4 cloves garlic, chopped

1 tsp. fresh ginger, finely chopped

2 medium tomatoes, peeled and chopped

1/4 cup lemon juice

1 tsp. ground cumin

1 tsp. ground allspice

1 Tbsp. vinegar

Place the lamb in the bottom of the cooking pan. In a large bowl, mix together the jalapeño peppers, green pepper, oil, onions, garlic, ginger, tomatoes, lemon juice, cumin, allspice and vinegar. Pour the sauce over the lamb. Cover and roast at 250°F for 2-3 hours, or until the lamb is tender and cooked to your preference. Serves 10.

Chapter 9

SEAFOOD & SHELLFISH ENTRÉES

Although fish and shellfish do not traditionally require a long cooking time, the moist method of roasting brings out their full flavor and cooks without drying the tender fish. Fish should flake easily when fully cooked and your Rival® Roaster Oven will easily roast fish and shellfish to your satisfaction. Try recipes such as *New Orleans Crab & Shrimp Casserole, Herb-Baked Salmon,* and *Mexican Crab Enchiladas* for excellent family dinners. And for a stellar meal, nothing can compare to the *Simple Lobster Dinner!*

COCONUT SHRIMP

Fresh from the tropics, serve these shrimp immediately after cooking.

2 lbs. shrimp (13–16 shrimp per lb.), peeled and deveined

1 tsp. black pepper

3/4 cup all-purpose flour

1 egg, well beaten

1/2 cup coconut, shredded

*To use in the 6, 8, or 10 quart Roaster Oven, decrease the recipe by half and use a 9" x 5" pan.

Preheat the Roaster Oven to 425°F. Lightly coat a 9" x 13" baking pan with cooking spray. Sprinkle the shrimp with the black pepper. Place the flour, egg and coconut in three separate bowls. Dip the shrimp in the flour one piece at a time, then the egg, and lastly the coconut and place in the baking pan. Repeat the process with all of the shrimp. Place the pan on the roasting rack in the cooking pan. Cover and bake for 12-15 minutes, or until the shrimp is golden brown and cooked through. Serves 12.

MEXICAN CRAB ENCHILADAS

2-10.75 oz. cans cream of mushroom soup

1 white onion, chopped

1/4 tsp. salt

1/2 tsp. black pepper

10 oz. frozen chopped spinach, thawed and drained

8 oz. crabmeat, fresh or canned, chopped

1 3/4 cups Monterey Jack cheese, shredded

6 corn tortillas

8 oz. evaporated milk

Southwest flavors meet fresh crab and spinach.

*To use in the 6, 8, or 10 quart Roaster Oven, decrease the recipe by half and use a 9" x 5" pan.

Lightly coat a 9" x 13" baking pan with nonstick spray. In a large bowl, combine 1 can of soup, onion, salt and black pepper. In another bowl, combine 1 can of the soup, the drained spinach, crab and cheese. Place ⅓ cup of the crab mixture on each tortilla and roll up, enchilada-style. Place the filled tortillas seam side down in the bottom of the baking pan. Stir the milk into the reserved soup and onion mixture and pour over the enchiladas. Place the baking pan on the roasting rack in the cooking pan. Cover and cook on 350°F for 30-45 minutes. Serves 8.

NEW ORLEANS CRAB & SHRIMP CASSEROLE

Too many delicious flavors to count! Use fresh crab and shrimp for best results.

6 Tbsp. butter or margarine, melted

1 cup white onion, chopped

1/2 cup scallions, chopped

2-10 oz. pkgs. frozen, chopped spinach, thawed and drained

10.75 oz. can cream of mushroom soup

3/4 cup Parmesan cheese, grated

14 oz. can marinated artichoke hearts

1/2 tsp. salt

1/2 tsp. white pepper

1/4 tsp. red pepper flakes

1 Tbsp. bottled hot sauce

1 lb. fresh crabmeat

1/2 lb. fresh shrimp, cooked

1 cup buttery crackers, crushed

*To use in the 6, 8, or 10 quart Roaster Oven, decrease the recipe by half and use a 9" x 5" pan.

Lightly coat a 9" x 13" baking pan with cooking spray and set aside. In a large frying pan over medium heat, sauté the onions and scallions in the butter until translucent in color. Add the spinach, soup and cheese. Reduce the heat and simmer until heated through. Add the artichoke hearts, salt, pepper, red pepper flakes and hot sauce. Simmer for 2-3 minutes. Gently fold in the crabmeat and shrimp. Pour the casserole into the baking pan and sprinkle the crackers over the top. Place the pan on the roasting rack in the cooking pan. Cover and cook at 350°F for 25-30 minutes. Serves 8.

SIMPLE LOBSTER DINNER

1 lb. uncooked lobster meat, cut into chunks

1 tsp. dry mustard

2 Tbsp. Old Bay™ seasoning

1 cup day-old bread, cubed

2 cups evaporated milk

1/4 tsp. salt

1/2 tsp. black pepper

Simple preparation, simply divine!

Lightly coat a 9" x 13" baking pan with cooking spray. Combine the lobster meat, mustard, seasoning, bread cubes, milk, salt and pepper in a large bowl. Stir and mix well. Pour the lobster casserole into the baking pan. Place the pan on the roasting rack in the cooking pan. Cover and cook at 350°F for 30-45 minutes. Serves 3-4.

*To use in the 6, 8, or 10 quart Roaster Oven, decrease the recipe by half and use a 9" x 5" pan.

145

HERB-BAKED SALMON

Salmon roasts to tender perfection!

4 salmon steaks, 1/2-inch thick

1 white onion, sliced

1 dried bay leaf

1/4 tsp. salt

1 Tbsp. lemon juice

2 cups water

4 Tbsp. bread crumbs

1 Tbsp. fresh parsley, chopped

4 cloves garlic, minced

3 Tbsp. butter, melted

*To use in the 6, 8, or 10 quart Roaster Oven, decrease the recipe by half and use a 9" x 5" pan.

Place the salmon in a 9" x 13" baking pan that has been coated with cooking spray. Add the onion, bay leaf, salt, lemon juice and the water and cover the salmon. Combine the bread crumbs, parsley, garlic and the melted butter in a small bowl. Sprinkle the herb crumb mixture equally on top of the salmon steaks. Place the baking pan on the roasting rack in the cooking pan. Cover and roast at 350°F for 25-35 minutes. Serves 4.

Chapter 10

MEATLESS MAIN DISHES

The recipes in this chapter for meatless meals have all the hearty goodness of a satisfying entrée but they do not contain meat. Some, such as *Spicy Macaroni & Cheese* and *Southwestern Black Bean & Cheddar Dinner,* include cheese as the source of protein, and others, such as *Spicy Lentils & Rice,* rely on legumes to add nutritional value. Whether you choose to use these dishes as accompaniments or as the main entrée of a meal we know that you'll discover some new favorites here.

SPICY MACARONI & CHEESE

Better than Mom's!

1 cup white onion, chopped

2 cloves garlic, minced

1/4 cup jalapeño peppers, chopped

1 tsp. ground coriander

1 1/2 tsp. ground cumin

1/2 cup unsalted butter, melted

1 lb. elbow macaroni, cooked and drained

1 cup salsa

10 3/4 oz. can cheddar cheese soup

1 1/2 cups cheddar cheese, grated

*This recipe can be doubled for the 18 or 20 quart Roaster Oven.

Lightly coat the cooking pan with nonstick cooking spray. In a large bowl, combine the onion, garlic, peppers, coriander, cumin and butter. Mix well to blend. Add the macaroni, salsa and cheese soup to the vegetables and spices and pour into the cooking pan. Cook at 300°F for 25-30 minutes. During the last 5 minutes of cooking, sprinkle the cheddar cheese on top. Serves 6-8.

MEDITERRANEAN VEGETABLES

2 large red onions, cut into 1/4-inch wedges

1 medium zucchini, sliced diagonally

1 yellow crookneck squash, sliced diagonally

1/4 cup olive oil

2 Tbsp. balsamic vinegar

1 Tbsp. fresh rosemary, chopped

Nonstick cooking spray

This tasty accompaniment to meat or poultry can also be served as a simple main dish.

Lightly spray the cooking pan with the nonstick cooking spray. In a large bowl, combine the onions, zucchini and squash with the olive oil and vinegar, making sure that all of the vegetables are coated with the oil and vinegar. Sprinkle the rosemary throughout the vegetables. Place the vegetables in the cooking pan. Cover and cook at 400°F for 45-60 minutes. Serve warm or allow to chill prior to serving. Serves 4.

PENNE WITH TOMATOES, BASIL & OLIVES

Italian cooking at its best—this dish is full of great flavor.

1 Tbsp. olive oil

I large yellow onion, chopped

3 cloves garlic, minced

28 oz. can whole tomatoes, chopped

2 cups chicken broth

2 Tbsp. fresh basil, chopped

1/2 tsp. ground oregano

1/2 tsp. black pepper

1 lb. penne pasta, cooked and drained

1 cup mozzarella cheese, shredded

1 cup pitted olives, cut in halves

1/2 cup Parmesan cheese, grated

*This recipe can be doubled for the 18 or 20 quart Roaster Oven.

In a saucepan, sauté the onion and garlic in the oil. Add the tomatoes, broth, basil, oregano and pepper and bring to a boil. Remove from the heat. Place the pasta, cheese and olives in the cooking pan and mix well. Pour the vegetables and herbs over the pasta and cook at 325°F for 30 minutes. Sprinkle the Parmesan cheese over the casserole before serving. Serves 6-8.

ZUCCHINI DELIGHT

1/2 cup extra virgin olive oil

28 oz. can whole tomatoes, crushed

2 red onions, sliced

5 zucchini squash, chopped

1 tsp. dried basil

1/4 tsp. salt

1/2 tsp. black pepper

1 1/2 cups mozzarella cheese, grated

1/2 cup Parmesan cheese, grated

Pour the olive oil into the bottom of the cooking pan. In a large bowl, combine the tomatoes, onions, zucchini, basil, salt and pepper. Pour the vegetables into the cooking pan and cook at 350°F 35-40 minutes. Just before serving, sprinkle the cheeses on top. Serves 6.

Use fresh zucchini from your garden!

*This recipe can be doubled for the 18 or 20 quart Roaster Oven.

SPAGHETTI & VEGGIE FRITTATA

A fun and nutritious entrée!

2 Tbsp. olive oil

1/2 lb. asparagus, trimmed and cut into 1-inch pieces, steamed until tender

8 oz. spaghetti, cooked and drained

1 yellow onion, sliced

1 yellow squash, thinly sliced

1 cup lowfat ricotta cheese

3 eggs, beaten

1/2 cup milk

1/4 tsp. salt

1/2 tsp. pepper

1/4 cup Parmesan cheese

This recipe can be doubled for the 18 or 20 quart Roaster Oven. Use a 9" x 9" baking pan.

Preheat the Roaster Oven to 350°F. Lightly coat a 5" x 7" loaf pan with the oil. In a large bowl, combine the asparagus, spaghetti, onion and squash. In a separate bowl, whisk the ricotta cheese, eggs and milk. Fold the cheese mixture into the spaghetti and vegetables. Place the frittata in the loaf pan and sprinkle with the salt, pepper and Parmesan cheese. Place the loaf pan in the cooking pan. Cover and cook for 35-40 minutes. Serves 6-8.

HEARTY BAKED PENNE

1 Tbsp. vegetable oil

1 white onion, chopped

2 large cloves garlic, chopped

28 oz. can seasoned tomatoes, diced

1/4 cup fresh basil, chopped

1 tsp. dried oregano, crumbled

1/2 cup Parmesan cheese, grated

15 oz. ricotta cheese

1 egg

1 1/2 cups mozzarella cheese, grated

16 oz. penne pasta, cooked and drained

Cheeses combine with herbs and pasta for a lovely meatless main dish. Add a fresh green salad and a baguette of bread for a complete meal.

Preheat the Roaster Oven to 400°F. Lightly coat a 9" x 13" baking dish with cooking spray. In a sauté pan, heat the oil over medium heat, add the onion and garlic and cook for 2-3 minutes. Add the tomatoes, basil and oregano and simmer for 5 minutes. In a medium bowl, combine the ricotta cheese and the egg. Reserve ¼ cup of the mozzarella cheese for the topping and add remaining mozzarella cheese to ricotta cheese and egg. Blend well. Spread a small amount of the tomato sauce over bottom of the pan. Layer ⅓ of the penne pasta over the sauce. Spoon ⅓ of the cheese mixture over the pasta. Spread ¼ cup of sauce over the cheese. Repeat the layers, using the remaining ingredients. On the final layer, sprinkle the reserved mozzarella and the ½ cup of Parmesan cheese. Place the baking dish on the roasting rack in the cooking pan. Cover and cook at 400°F for 30-40 minutes, or until heated through. Serves 8-10.

153

SOUTHWESTERN BLACK BEAN & CHEDDAR DINNER

Accompany this dish with restaurant-style tortilla chips and add salsa and sour cream as garnishes.

1 Tbsp. olive oil

1 cup white onion, chopped

1 1/2 cups yellow cornmeal

2 Tbsp. chili powder

8 oz. evaporated milk

15 oz. can black beans, rinsed and drained

1 cup whole kernel corn

28 oz. can stewed tomatoes

1 cup cheddar cheese, shredded

*This recipe can be doubled for the 18 or 20 quart Roaster Oven.

Lightly coat the cooking pan with cooking spray. In a large bowl, combine the oil, onion, cornmeal, chili powder, milk, beans, corn and tomatoes and mix well. Spoon the casserole into the cooking pan. Cook on 300°F for 45-60 minutes. During the last 5 minutes of cooking, sprinkle the cheese on top. Serves 4.

SPICY LENTILS & RICE

6 oz. can tomato paste

1.25 oz. pkg. taco seasoning mix

1 Tbsp. chili powder

1 cup lentils, cooked

1 cup white onion, chopped

1 cup green bell pepper, chopped

1 cup celery, chopped

3 cups water

1 1/2 cups converted rice

There's nothing shy about these lentils! Taco and chili flavors combine to partner with the mild and slightly sweet lentils.

In a large bowl, blend together the tomato paste, taco seasoning and chili powder. Add the lentils, onion, pepper and celery and mix well. Add the water and rice and combine thoroughly until well blended. Spoon the lentils and vegetables into the cooking pan. Cook at 200°F for 1½ hours. Serves 4.

*This recipe can be doubled for the 18 or 20 quart Roaster Oven.

GREEK SPINACH PIE

Feta cheese, dill and spinach create a classic Greek dish!

6 eggs

10 oz. frozen, chopped spinach, defrosted and drained

3/4 lb. Feta cheese, crumbled

1 cup leeks, diced (white part only)

1/4 cup fresh dill, chopped

1 tsp. pepper, freshly ground

8 sheets phyllo pastry

1/2 cup butter, melted

*Use a small loaf pan and decrease the recipe by half when using the 6, 8 or 10 quart Roaster Oven.

Preheat the Roaster Oven to 375°F. Butter a 7" x 11" baking dish. In a large bowl, beat the eggs until fluffy and fold in the spinach, feta cheese, leeks, dill and pepper. Layer a sheet of phyllo into the baking dish and brush the sheet lightly with butter. Repeat the process with another 4 sheets, turning each sheet slightly so that the corners fan out (try to avoid stacking each sheet directly on top of another). Brush each sheet with melted butter. Reserve 3 sheets of phyllo pastry. Pour the spinach mixture into the prepared sheets and fold the pastry ends over the spinach. Butter the reserved sheets of phyllo and place them on top to cover the pan, folding in the edges. Place the baking dish on the roasting rack in the cooking pan. Cover and cook at 375°F for 45-55 minutes, or until golden brown. Serves 6.

SLICED POTATO & MOZZARELLA BAKE

1 Tbsp. vegetable oil

5 large baking potatoes, peeled and cut in thin slices

4 large, beefsteak tomatoes, seeded, sliced and drained

1 white onion, sliced

1/2 tsp. dried oregano

1/2 tsp. dried basil

1 tsp. salt

1/2 tsp. white pepper

2 cups whole milk mozzarella cheese, grated

1/3 cup Parmesan cheese, grated

1/4 cup butter, cut into bits

Lightly coat the cooking pan with the vegetable oil. Layer one-half of the potatoes, tomatoes and onion in the cooking pan. Season the vegetables with the one-half of the oregano, basil, salt and pepper and sprinkle with half of each of the cheeses. Repeat the layers with the remaining half of the ingredients. Dot the top of the casserole with the butter. Cover and cook on 350°F for 45-60 minutes. Serves 6.

Cheeses and herbs enhance this any-day-of-the-week dinner!

This recipe can be doubled for the 18 or 20 quart Roaster Oven.

Chapter 11

HEALTHY FOODS FOR A HEALTHY LIFESTYLE

With the right preparation and a handful of fresh herbs and spices you can delight in some very scrumptious foods—even if they are low in fat and calories. Because roasting adds moisture you can prepare lower-fat cuts of beef and pork without losing tenderness. Your Rival® Roaster Oven will capture the flavor of all the light sauces and marinades you use in preparation.

Savory Sage Pork Tenderloin, Chicken & Mushroom Fusilli and *Italian Basil Roast* are just a few recipes that bring the best flavors together with the healthiest eating choices. Included in this chapter are nutritional analyses for each recipe, so whether you are adopting new eating patterns or simply looking for a healthy meal you'll know just how good these dishes are for you.

LEMON BASIL SHRIMP & RICE

Light, yet full of flavor.

2 Tbsp. olive oil

3 lbs. fresh shrimp, shelled and deveined

1/2 cup diet margarine, melted

3 tsp. garlic, minced

1 Tbsp. fresh lemon juice

1 Tbsp. fresh basil, minced

6 cups hot, cooked rice

Calories:	339
Total Fat:	7 gm.
Saturated Fat:	> 1 gm.
Carbohydrates:	30 gm.
Protein:	38 gm.
Cholesterol:	259 mg.
Sodium:	346 mg.

Spread the oil in the bottom of the cooking pan. In a small bowl, toss the shrimp, butter, garlic, lemon juice and basil. Spread the shrimp mixture evenly in the bottom of the cooking pan. Cover and cook at 350°F for 25-35 minutes, or until the shrimp turn pink and are cooked through. To serve, arrange equal portions of shrimp over the hot rice and drizzle any remaining sauce over the shrimp. Serves 8.

This recipe can be doubled for the 18 or 20 quart Roaster Oven.

160

CHICKEN & MUSHROOM FUSILLI

4 cups lowfat chicken broth

3 cups fresh crimini mushrooms, quartered

2 lbs. boneless, skinless chicken breasts, cubed

1 medium white onion, diced

2 Tbsp. sesame oil

2 Tbsp. sherry

2 Tbsp. fresh parsley, chopped

1/4 tsp. salt

1/2 tsp. black pepper

1 lb. hot, cooked fusilli pasta (or other shapes of your choice)

Crimini mushrooms are the perfect complement to the chicken and pasta.

Combine the chicken broth, mushrooms and chicken in the cooking pan of the Roaster Oven and cover. Heat the Roaster Oven to 350°F. Allow the chicken and broth to reach a full boil. Reduce the heat to 200°F and add the onion, sesame oil, sherry, parsley, salt and pepper. Cover and allow the stew to simmer for 15-25 minutes, stirring often. To serve, ladle equal portions of the chicken and mushrooms over individual bowls of the cooked pasta. Serves 6.

This recipe can be doubled for the 18 or 20 quart Roaster Oven.

Calories:	379
Total Fat:	8 gm.
Saturated Fat:	2 gm.
Carbohydrates:	27 gm.
Protein:	44 gm.
Cholesterol:	88 mg.
Sodium:	854 mg.

ITALIAN-HERBED OVEN FRIES

This is a healthy and delicious way to enjoy fries. They are baked without fat and are full of exciting flavors.

1 1/2 lbs. baking potatoes, peeled
nonstick cooking spray
1/4 cup Parmesan cheese, grated
1 tsp. ground oregano
1/2 tsp. ground rosemary
1/4 tsp. black pepper
1/4 tsp. salt (optional)

Calories:	75
Total Fat:	2 gm.
Saturated Fat:	1 gm.
Carbohydrates:	10 gm.
Protein:	6 gm.
Cholesterol:	5 mg.
Sodium:	129 mg.

Cut the potatoes lengthwise into ¼-inch slices and then cut the slices into ¼" wide sticks. Place the potatoes in a large bowl and lightly spray with the nonstick cooking spray. Toss to coat. Add the remaining ingredients and toss to coat thoroughly. Transfer the potato mixture to the cooking pan. Cover and cook at 400°F for 40 minutes, turning the potatoes every 10 minutes, or until they are golden brown and crisp. Sprinkle with salt, if desired. Serves 4.

For the 6, 8 or 10 quart Roaster Oven, decrease the recipe by half.

BAKED CITRUS FISH

1 lb. mild, white fish fillets

1/4 tsp. salt

1/2 tsp. black pepper

1 white onion, chopped

5 Tbsp. fresh parsley, chopped

2 Tbsp. extra-virgin olive oil

2 tsp. lemon rind, grated

2 tsp. orange rind, grated

1 cup orange juice

1/2 cup lemon juice

Use filet of sole, red snapper or any other seasonal white fish.

Salt and pepper the fish. Place the fillets in a 9" x 13" pan and sprinkle the onion over each fillet. In a medium bowl, mix together the parsley, oil, lemon rind, orange rind, orange juice and lemon juice. Pour the sauce over the fillets. Place the baking pan on the roasting rack in the cooking pan. Cover and roast at 325°F for 25-30 minutes, or until the fish flakes easily and is cooked through. Serves 3-4.

*Decrease the recipe by half and use a small loaf pan when using the 6, 8 or 10 quart Roaster Oven.

Calories:	261
Total Fat:	14 gm.
Saturated Fat:	1 gm.
Carbohydrates:	12 gm.
Protein:	23 gm.
Cholesterol:	68 mg.
Sodium:	101 mg.

SUMMER SQUASH SOUP

Substitute other seasonal summer vegetables for a light dinner or luncheon meal.

2 Tbsp. diet margarine, melted

4 medium yellow squash, cut into small chunks

1/2 tsp. garlic salt

1/2 tsp. salt

1/2 tsp. black pepper

1 tsp. dried rosemary

3 cups lowfat chicken broth

1 cup water

2 cups cooked boneless, skinless chicken breasts, cubed

Calories:	203
Total Fat:	6 gm.
Saturated Fat:	2 gm.
Carbohydrates:	11 gm.
Protein:	26 gm.
Cholesterol:	60 mg.
Sodium:	894 mg.

Preheat the Roaster Oven to 375°F. Combine the butter and squash in the cooking pan and cook the squash for 5 minutes, stirring often. Add the garlic salt, salt, pepper, rosemary, chicken broth, water, and chicken. Stir well to mix. Cover and reduce the temperature to 250°F. Simmer the soup for 15 minutes and serve warm. Serves 3-4.

This recipe can be doubled for the 18 or 20 quart Roaster Oven.

ITALIAN BASIL ROAST

4 lbs. boneless top round roast

2 Tbsp. extra-virgin olive oil

1/4 cup lemon juice

3 Tbsp. dried basil,

1 Tbsp. garlic powder

1/4 tsp. salt

1/2 tsp. black pepper

1 medium white onion, cut into thin slices

When eating beef, choose less fatty cuts of beef and eat 4-6 oz. portions.

Remove all visible fat from the roast. Using a sharp knife make cuts ½-inch in depth over the entire roast. In a small bowl, whisk together the oil, lemon juice, basil, garlic powder, salt and pepper. Place the roast on the roasting rack in the cooking pan and pour the sauce over the roast. Layer the onions over the sauce. Cover and roast at 325°F for 48-60 minutes, or until the roast is tender and cooked to your preference. To serve, cut into thin slices. Serves 12-16.

Calories:	218
Total Fat:	12 gm.
Saturated Fat:	4 gm.
Carbohydrates:	2 gm.
Protein:	26 gm.
Cholesterol:	67 mg.
Sodium:	68 mg.

*This recipe can be doubled for the 18 quart or 20 quart Roaster Oven, but increase the cooking time based on 12-20 minutes per pound of beef roasting at 325°F.

SAVORY SAGE PORK TENDERLOIN

Pork tenderloin is especially good when roasted and the fat content is lower than other cuts of pork.

1 cup fresh sage, minced

1/4 tsp. salt

1/2 tsp. black pepper

1/2 cup fresh lemon juice

2 Tbsp. lowfat margarine, melted

4 lbs. pork tenderloin

Calories:	173
Total Fat:	7 gm.
Saturated Fat:	2 gm.
Carbohydrates:	2 gm.
Protein:	23 gm.
Cholesterol:	75 mg.
Sodium:	74 mg.

Remove all visible fat from the pork tenderloin. Combine the sage, salt and pepper, lemon juice and margarine in a bowl. Use a sharp knife to make slices ¼-inch in depth over the entire tenderloin. Place the pork tenderloin on the roasting rack in the cooking pan. Pour the sauce over the pork. Cover and roast for 1 ½-2 hours, or until tender and cooked to your preference. Allow the tenderloin to cool for 15 minutes before slicing. Serves 16.

RASPBERRY & SHALLOT CHICKEN

2 Tbsp. lowfat margarine, melted

6 boneless, skinless chicken breasts

2/3 cup raspberry vinegar

2 Tbsp. shallots or onion, chopped

This surprisingly elegant entrée is very light in fat and calories. For extra flavor, try marinating the chicken in the sauce for 2-6 hours before roasting.

Spread the margarine in the bottom of the cooking pan. Place the chicken breasts on top of the margarine. Pour the raspberry vinegar over the chicken and sprinkle the shallots on top. Cover and roast at 350°F for 35-45 minutes, or until the chicken is tender and cooked to the correct internal temperature. Serves 6.

Calories:	107
Total Fat:	2 gm.
Saturated Fat:	>1 gm.
Carbohydrates:	3 gm.
Protein:	16 gm.
Cholesterol:	41 mg.
Sodium:	71 mg.

Chapter 12

DESSERTS FOR ALL OCCASIONS

If you've never thought about preparing your dessert in the Rival® Roaster Oven take a look at the wonderful recipes in this chapter—*Southern Pecan Pie,* chock-full of pecans and rich sweetness, *Thanksgiving Day Pumpkin Pie,* a traditional and timeless dessert, and *Duo-Berry Crisp,* combining fresh berries with cinnamon and sugar!

In addition to pies and fruit crisps, the Rival® Roaster Oven also bakes such delights as moist nut and fruit breads—*Walnut & Apple Loaf* and *Blueberry Poppy Seed Bread.* Try these wonderful desserts, whether you are looking for a bit of something sweet or preparing desserts for a crowd. They're all sure to impress!

APPLE BROWN BETTY

This yummy dessert has been a favorite choice of families for over one hundred years.

3 Tbsp. butter or margarine, melted

1 1/2 cups soft bread crumbs

1/2 cup brown sugar

1 tsp. ground cinnamon

1/8 tsp. ground nutmeg

2 cups Golden Delicious apples, peeled and sliced

*This recipe can be doubled for the 18 or 20 quart Roaster Oven, using 2 loaf pans.

Preheat the Roaster Oven to 350°F. Coat a 9" x 5" loaf pan with butter. In a small bowl, toss the bread crumbs with the butter. In a large bowl, combine the sugar, cinnamon, and nutmeg and blend well. Add the apples and gently toss thoroughly to make sure they are coated evenly. Place ½ cup of the bread crumbs in the loaf pan. Layer half of the apples on top. Continue making layers until the bread crumbs and apples are all layered in the loaf pan. Cover the pan with aluminum foil. Place the pan on the roasting rack in the cooking pan. Cover and bake for 25 minutes. Remove the aluminum foil and bake for an additional 25 minutes. Serve while warm. Serves 6.

BLUEBERRY POPPY SEED BREAD

2 cups all purpose flour

1/2 cup sugar

1 Tbsp. baking powder

2 Tbsp. poppy seeds

1/2 tsp. salt

1 egg

1 cup milk

1/4 cup vegetable oil

3/4 cup fresh blueberries, (you may substitute frozen, thawed blueberries, if desired)

Is this a dessert or a bread? Tender and sweet and full of blueberry flavor!

This recipe can be doubled for the 18 or 20 quart Roaster Oven, using 2 loaf pans.

Preheat the Roaster Oven to 400°F. Coat a 9" x 5" loaf pan with cooking spray. In a large bowl, mix with a fork the flour, sugar, baking powder, poppy seeds and salt. In a separate bowl, beat the egg slightly with a fork and then add the milk and oil to the egg. Add the egg mixture to the flour mixture and blend until the flour is moistened. Gently fold in the blueberries. Spoon the batter into the loaf pan. Place the loaf pan on the roasting rack in the cooking pan. Cover and bake for 35-45 minutes or until a toothpick inserted in the center comes out clean. Immediately remove the bread from the pan and cool on a wire rack before slicing. Serves 8.

BASIC PASTRY CRUST

A classic crust for all pie recipes.

1 cup all-purpose flour
1/2 tsp. salt
1/3 cup shortening, chilled
3 Tbsp. water (approximately)

Sift the flour. Measure out 1 cup and add the salt. Using a pastry blender or two knives, cut the shortening into the flour and salt to form crumbs the size of peas. Add the water while mixing lightly with a fork. Use no more water than is needed to hold the pastry together. Shape the dough into a ball, handling as little as possible. Chill the dough for 1 hour.

Roll out the dough on a lightly floured surface until it is evenly ⅛-inch thick and 2" larger than a 9-inch pie pan. Transfer the dough to the pie pan, pressing the pastry lightly against the sides of the pan. Avoid stretching the dough (note: pastry that is stretched will shrink during baking). Leave edges around the pie about ½-inch larger than the pan. Turn under ½-inch of the pastry and flute the edges by pressing the forefinger of one hand between the thumb and forefinger of the other hand along the entire edge of the pie. Yields 1 9-inch Pie.

172

SOUTHERN PECAN PIE

3 eggs

3/4 cup sugar

3/4 cup dark corn syrup

2 Tbsp. butter, melted

2 tsp. vanilla extract

2 Tbsp. all-purpose flour

1/2 tsp. salt

1 cup shelled pecans halves

9-inch Basic Pastry Crust

The quintessential taste of the South. Serve with whipped cream.

For the 6, 8, or 10 quart Roaster Oven, use 3" tart pans or individual pie shells.

With an electric mixer, beat the eggs until thoroughly mixed. Continue beating and add the sugar, corn syrup, butter, vanilla extract, flour and salt. Pour the filling mixture into the pastry-lined pie pan. Place the pecans evenly on top of the pie, covering the top of the pie as much as possible. Bake in the Roaster Oven in the center of the rack at 450°F for 20 minutes. Do not open the lid of the roaster while baking. Reduce the temperature to 425°F and bake for approximately 30-35 minutes, or until the pie is set and the pastry is lightly browned. Serve while warm or cool and refrigerate any leftover pie. Serves 6-8.

FAVORITE CUSTARD PIE

As a variation, top with seasonal fruit or homemade jam.

4 eggs, beaten
1/2 cup sugar
1/4 tsp. salt
2 1/2 cups milk
1 tsp. vanilla extract
1 tsp. nutmeg
9–inch Basic Pastry Crust

Preheat the Roaster Oven to 425°F. Prepare the pastry crust as directed. Beat the eggs until very well blended and add the sugar and salt. Scald the milk and cool slightly. Add the milk to the egg mixture and stir in the vanilla extract. Blend again. Pour the pie into the pie shell and sprinkle with nutmeg. Place the pie on the roasting rack in the cooking pan. Cover and bake at 475°F for 10 minutes. Reduce the heat to 425°F for 15-25 minutes, or until the pie is just firm. Serve while warm or cool and refrigerate any leftover pie. Serves 8.

THANKSGIVING DAY PUMPKIN PIE

1 cup pumpkin, canned or freshly cooked

1/2 cup sugar

1/2 tsp. salt

1 tsp. ground ginger

1/2 tsp. ground nutmeg

1 tsp. ground cinnamon

2 eggs, beaten

1 cup light cream

9-inch Basic Pastry Crust

The perfect pie for your Thanksgiving Day meal. As the spices bake, a mouth-watering fragrance fills the air.

Preheat the Roaster Oven to 425°F. Prepare the pastry crust as directed. In a large bowl, mix together the pumpkin, sugar, salt, ginger, nutmeg and cinnamon. Add the beaten eggs and cream and blend well again. Pour the pie into the pastry-lined pie pan. Place the pie on the roasting rack in the cooking pan. Cover and bake for 10 minutes. Reduce the temperature to 325°F and cook for an additional 30-40 minutes or until the center of the pie is firm. Serves 8.

FRESH APPLE CRANBERRY PIE

The marriage of apples and cranberries produces this delicious pie.

5 red baking apples (any variety), peeled and sliced

1 1/2 cups fresh cranberries

1 cup sugar

2 Tbsp. flour

1 tsp. ground nutmeg

1 tsp. ground cinnamon

9-inch Basic Pastry Crust

Preheat the Roaster Oven to 450°F. Combine the apples, cranberries, sugar, flour, nutmeg and cinnamon and blend well. Spoon the pie into the prepared pie crust. Place the pie on the roasting rack in the cooking pan. Cover and bake for 10 minutes. Reduce the heat to 375°F and bake for an additional 35-40 minutes, or until the fruit is tender. Serves 6-8.

DUO-BERRY CRISP

2 cups fresh blueberries (you may substitute frozen, thawed blueberries, if preferred)

2 cups fresh raspberries (you may substitute frozen, thawed raspberries, if preferred)

3/4 cup sugar

2 Tbsp. cornstarch

2 Tbsp. fresh lemon juice

1/2 cup rolled oats, regular or instant

1/2 cup flour

1/2 cup brown sugar

3/4 cup butter or margarine

Substitute blackberries, boysenberries or other seasonal favorites.

Preheat the Roaster Oven to 375°F. Lightly coat a 9" x 5" loaf pan with cooking spray. In a small bowl, combine the berries, sugar, cornstarch and lemon juice. Toss lightly to coat the berries. In another bowl, combine the rolled oats, flour, brown sugar and butter. Sprinkle ½ cup of the berry mixture on the bottom of the loaf pan. Cover the berries with ¼ cup of the oat crisp. Repeat the layers, alternating berries and the crisp mixture. Place the loaf pan on the roasting rack in the cooking pan. Cover and bake for 40-55 minutes. Serves 6.

*To use an 18 or 20 quart Roaster Oven, place a 9" x 13" pan over the roasting rack. You may also use 2 loaf pans on the roasting rack.

177

WALNUT & APPLE LOAF

Dense and moist— and full of cinnamon and nutmeg flavors.

*To use an 18 or 20 quart Roaster Oven, place a 9" x 13" pan over the roasting rack. You may also use 2 loaf pans over the roasting rack.

1/2 cup butter or margarine, melted

3/4 cup light brown sugar

1/2 cup granulated sugar

3 eggs

1/4 cup sour cream

1 banana, mashed

2 tsp. vanilla extract

2 cups flour

1 tsp. baking powder

1/2 tsp. ground cinnamon

1/4 tsp. ground nutmeg

2 Golden Delicious apples, cored, peeled and chopped (you may substitute another variety of baking apples, if preferred)

1 cup walnuts, chopped

Preheat the Roaster Oven to 350°F. Lightly coat a 9" x 5" loaf pan with cooking spray. In a large bowl, mix together the butter, brown sugar, granulated sugar and beat in the eggs. When well-blended, stir in the sour cream, banana and vanilla extract. In a separate bowl, combine the flour, baking powder, cinnamon and nutmeg. Gently fold the flour mixture into the batter. Fold in the apples and chopped walnuts. Spoon the batter into the loaf pan. Place the loaf on roasting rack in the cooking pan. Cover and bake for 45-60 minutes, or until a toothpick comes out clean when placed in the center. Serves 8.

APRICOT BREAD

2 cups all-purpose flour

1 Tbsp. baking powder

1 cup brown sugar

1/4 cup butter or margarine, melted

1 egg

1/3 cup water

1 cup dried apricots, diced

Dried apricots give this bread just the right amount of sweetness.

Preheat the Roaster Oven to 350°F. Grease a 9" x 5" loaf pan with butter or nonstick cooking spray. In a large bowl, mix together the flour and baking powder. In another bowl, blend the brown sugar, butter, egg and water. Stir the butter mixture into the flour mixture in small batches. Mix just enough to blend all ingredients. Fold in the apricots. Place the pan on the roasting rack in the cooking pan. Bake at 350°F for 35-50 minutes, or until a toothpick inserted in the center comes out clean. Cool before slicing. Serves 8.

*To use an 18 or 20 quart Roaster Oven, place a 9" x 13" pan over the roasting rack. You may also use 2 loaf pans over the roasting rack.

179

BANANA NUT BREAD

A cook's favorite and an all-time crowd-pleaser.

3 1/2 cups flour

3 tsp. baking powder

1 tsp. salt

3/4 cup butter or margarine

1 1/2 cups sugar

4 eggs, beaten

3 tsp. vanilla extract

6 ripe bananas, chopped

1/2 cup walnuts, chopped (optional)

Preheat the Roaster Oven to 350°F. Lightly coat two 9" x 5" loaf pans (or one 9" x 13" baking pan) with cooking spray or butter. Sift together the flour, baking powder and salt. In another bowl, cream the butter and sugar together until they are light and creamy in color. Add the eggs and vanilla extract to the butter and sugar. Fold the batter into the flour mixture until blended. Add the bananas and mix again. Spoon the batter into the loaf pans. If adding walnuts, sprinkle them on top of the bread and place the loaf pans on the roasting rack in the cooking pan. Cover and bake for 55-65 minutes or until a toothpick inserted in the center of the loaves comes out clean. Cool before slicing. Serves 8-10.

CHOCOLATE CHIP PIE

1 cup sugar

2 eggs

1/2 cup butter or margarine, melted

1/4 cup cornstarch

1/4 cup water

2 Tbsp. vanilla extract

6 oz. chocolate chips

9-inch Basic Pastry Crust

Serve this rich pie in small pieces for a superb ending to any meal.

Preheat the Roaster Oven to 350°F. In a large bowl, mix together the sugar, eggs, and butter. Blend the cornstarch, water and vanilla extract in a small cup. Add the cornstarch mixture to the egg mixture and blend well. When blended, gently fold the chocolate chips into the batter. Pour the batter into the pastry-lined pie pan. Place the pie on the roasting rack in the cooking pan. Cover and bake at 350°F for 45-50 minutes, or until a knife inserted in the center comes out clean. Serves 8-10.

FRESH PEACH & BLUEBERRY COBBLER

Substitute any seasonal fruit, if desired. Choose from peaches, apples, blueberries and raspberries. Yummy!

1/2 cup butter or margarine

1 1/4 cups sugar

1 egg, beaten

1 tsp. vanilla extract

3/4 cup fresh blueberries, cleaned and drained

3/4 cup fresh peaches, diced

1 cup all-purpose flour

1 tsp. baking soda

1/2 tsp. ground cinnamon

Optional: 1/2 cup of nuts of your choice may be sprinkled on the cobbler before baking. You may also substitute any other flavoring extracts for the vanilla extract.

Preheat the Roaster Oven to 325°F. In a large bowl, cream the butter and sugar until fluffy and light in color. Add the egg and vanilla extract and beat well. Add the fruit and stir gently. Pour the batter into a loaf pan. In a small bowl, sift together the flour, baking soda and cinnamon. Spoon the flour mixture over the top of the batter. Place the pan on the roasting rack in the cooking pan. Cover and bake for 35-40 minutes, or until the center of the cobbler is set. Serve warm or cool. Serves 8.

PEAR & APPLE BREAD PUDDING

2 cups milk

1 cup sugar

4 large eggs

1/2 cup butter, melted

4 cups bread, cubed

1 large apple, peeled, cored, and diced

1 large pear, cored and diced

1 cup raisins

A tender and delicious old-fashioned dessert.

Preheat the Roaster Oven to 350°F. Lightly grease a 9" x 13" baking pan. In a large bowl, blend the milk, sugar, eggs and butter together. When well combined, fold the bread, apple, pear and raisins into the egg mixture. Pour the pudding into the baking pan. Place the baking pan on the roasting rack in the cooking pan. Cover and cook for 45-60 minutes, or until the center is set. Serves 8-12.

Decrease the recipe by half and use a small loaf pan when using the 6, 8 or 10 quart Roaster Oven.

183

DREAMY CASHEW BARS

Total decadence!

3/4 cup butter, softened

1 1/4 cups light brown sugar

2 tsp. vanilla

2 eggs

2 cups all-purpose flour

2 tsp. baking powder

1 1/2 cups cashews, chopped

1 1/2 cups chocolate chips

Decrease the recipe by half and use a small loaf pan when using the 6, 8 or 10 quart Roaster Oven.

Preheat the Roaster Oven to 350°F. Lightly grease a 9" x 13" baking pan. In a large bowl, combine the butter and sugar. Add the vanilla and eggs; beating with an electric mixer on low speed until blended. Add the flour and baking powder and beat again until well combined. Stir in 1 cup each of the nuts and chocolate chips. Spread the dough evenly in the baking pan. Sprinkle with the remaining nuts and chocolate chips. Place the baking pan on the roasting rack in the cooking pan. Cover and cook for 45-55 minutes. Cool before cutting. Makes 20 bars.

RICH CHOCOLATE & CARMEL BARS

2 cups graham cracker crumbs

1/2 cup butter, melted

12 oz. can condensed milk

30 individually wrapped caramels, unwrapped

12 oz. chocolate chips

1 cup crispy rice cereal

2 cups walnuts, chopped

2 Tbsp. vanilla extract

The crunch of krispy rice cereal offers a delicious contrast to creamy caramel.

*Decrease the recipe by half and use a small loaf pan when using the 6, 8 or 10 quart Roaster Oven.

Preheat the Roaster Oven to 350°F. In a small bowl, combine the graham cracker crumbs and butter. Press the crumbs evenly in the bottom of a 9" x 13" baking dish. Place the baking dish on the roasting rack in the cooking pan. Cover and cook for 15 minutes. In a small saucepan over low heat, combine the milk and caramels. Stir until the caramels melt. Remove from the heat and allow to cool for at least 10 minutes. Sprinkle the chocolate chips, rice cereal and walnuts over the graham cracker crust. Stir the vanilla extract into the milk and caramels. Drizzle the milk and caramel sauce over the graham cracker crust. Place the baking dish back on the roasting rack in the cooking pan. Cover and cook for 20-25 minutes. Cool completely before cutting into bars. Makes 20 bars.

BAKED BANANA DELIGHT

Serve warm with a large scoop of vanilla ice cream.

1/4 cup butter, melted

1/4 cup packed light brown sugar

2 Tbsp. lemon juice

1/4 cup orange juice

1 tsp. ground cinnamon

6 medium bananas, peeled and sliced into 1-inch pieces

*Decrease the recipe by half and use a small loaf pan when using the 6, 8 or 10 quart Roaster Oven.

Preheat the Roaster Oven to 375°F. Spread the butter over a 9" x 13" baking pan. In a large bowl, combine the sugar, lemon juice, orange juice and cinnamon. Add the bananas and completely coat all the banana pieces evenly. Pour the mixture into the baking pan. Place the baking pan on the roasting rack in the cooking pan. Cover and cook for 15-25 minutes.

MINI APPLE PIZZA

10 oz. refrigerator biscuits

1/2 cup brown sugar

2 Tbsp. flour

1 tsp. ground cinnamon

2 apples, peeled and shredded

This easy dessert is loved by everyone!

Lightly grease a 9" x 13" baking dish. Pat the biscuits into flat circles about 3" wide. Place the biscuits in the baking dish. In a mixing bowl, combine the brown sugar, flour and cinnamon; mix well. Add the apples and mix again. Spoon rounded tablespoonfuls of the spiced apples onto each biscuit. Place the baking dish on the roasting rack in the cooking pan. Cover and cook at 350°F for 25-40 minutes.

*Decrease the recipe by half and use a small loaf pan when using the 6, 8 or 10 quart Roaster Oven.

187

Personal Notes

FOOD	ROASTING TEMPERATURE	ROASTING TIME

FOOD	ROASTING TEMPERATURE	ROASTING TIME

Personal Notes

FOOD	ROASTING TEMPERATURE	ROASTING TIME

FOOD	ROASTING TEMPERATURE	ROASTING TIME

INDEX